FIFTY
isn't
Fatal Anymore

FIFTY
isn't
Fatal Anymore

Mary Christofano

iUniverse, Inc.
New York Lincoln Shanghai

FIFTY isn't Fatal Anymore

iUniverse books may be ordered through booksellers or by contacting:

iUniverse
2021 Pine Lake Road, Suite 100
Lincoln, NE 68512
www.iuniverse.com
1-800-Authors (1-800-288-4677)

I am writing this book as an individual who is over fifty years old, based upon my actual experiences. I am not a physician, health expert, nutritionist, fitness trainer, or psychiatrist. I talk about things that have worked for me, ideas I have read about and what has worked for other people I know. Before you make any changes in your diet, exercise routine, skin care or health care, please consult your physician. This is vital to your safety and well-being. Not every diet, exercise or makeup routine works for everyone. Keep this in mind as you read this book. Check with a dermatologist and test all makeup and skin care products per the package directions before using.

ISBN: 978-0-595-41703-2 (pbk)
ISBN: 978-0-595-86046-3 (ebk)

Printed in the United States of America

Contents

FOREWORD

This book is being written as homage to the *baby boomer* generation whose motto is; *never grow old.* It is such an interesting dichotomy that even though our generation is aging, we have a different attitude toward it and we think younger than any other generation before us.

I often wonder why this is so. It seems that we are a bit skeptical as a group to begin with and we are rebellious, challenge authority and don't buy into what always has been and will be. This sets us apart from other generations in both our thinking and actions. We are more accepting of differences in culture, diversity, attitude and open to new ideas about everything.

This gives us the audacity and ego that is representative of our refusal to age and grow up. We cling to our youthfulness in every way possible. Just look at the rise in the popularity of plastic surgery, diet crazes, fitness obsessions and even pills for everything from staying "hard" to cleaning arteries, keeping skin younger looking and growing hair!

With this in mind, I have decided to explore many aspects of growing older and just plain living life and all it entails and at the same time thinking and feeling younger and hope it can be beneficial to those who seek everlasting youthfulness and fulfillment in body, mind and spirit.

In this book, I share my ideas and some helpful things I have learned over the years in the areas of attitude, health, exercise, success, relationships, living your dream, finances, beauty, hobbies, stress reduction, living in the moment, having adventures and never taking anything for granted. Hopefully you will find something that sparks energy in your life from my work and if that happens then you have made my day.

This book is both for men and women and for anyone interested in living a full and happy life. It is not just for baby boomers, but for every generation.

INTRODUCTION

Our generation does not want to age and we refuse to give in to the adage that just because we are advancing in years doesn't mean we have to be …

- Not cool
- Overweight
- Must dress conservatively
- Must accept less important job positions
- Must be put out to pasture
- Must not dare to dream
- Must give up the hope for new love or a bright future
- Must sit back in our rocking chairs and give up
- Must have nothing but health problems and aches and pains
- Must be depressed
- Must give up on finding a partner
- Must have less money
- Must be belittled, frowned upon and pitied by the young
- Must fear the future
- Must regret the past

What you do with your middle years and beyond is entirely up to you. Your future is as bright as you decide to make it. There are no limits except those that you place upon yourself with outdated ideas of what is supposed to happen as we age. Guard yourself from any of these negative thoughts.

From today forward your commitment to creating a healthful, happy, productive, less stressful and exhilarating life is in your hands. Make the most of it and appreciate the wonderful gift our advancing years present to us.

In this book I present ideas and practices that I use for diet and exercise. I am not a physician or health advisor. Please always check with your doctor or health practitioner before you make any changes in your diet or exercise program.

1
ATTITUDE

Many times, as I grew older people would come up to me and say that I didn't look my age. They would usually guess it at least ten years younger. This was always a pleasant surprise to me. Now that I am over fifty years of age, I hear this even more often. It is due in a good part to genetics, but in a large part to attitude, taking care of myself and also my refusal to buy into the mindset that getting older means anything negative. Going downhill is not a phrase in my guidebook and shouldn't be in yours. Our advancing ages should be the best of our lives.

"Eighteen 'til I die," is a line from a Bryan Adams song that keeps playing in my head. (Adams, Bryan CD) Attitude toward aging plays a huge part in how you approach the middle years and beyond. I refuse to accept the idea that just because the years are advancing, we have to let ourselves go. The face may get wrinkles, but we can still keep our bodies youthful and taut with exercise and good eating habits.

We baby boomers are the generation who will be *challenging* the aging process and changing the old negative attitudes of others by setting the example. We will show that you can maintain your attractiveness, health and body shape well into your advancing years.

When I first moved to Naples, Florida over ten years ago, I was very impressed by the superb shape of some of the older adults. One gentleman in his eighties would swim for miles in the gulf everyday. He would get out of the water and his body was tanned and toned and his energy was incredible. I was impressed by his positive, ebullient presence. He was very attractive and he knew it. He still thought of himself as a *lady-killer* and he definitely was!

Another resident was a woman, probably in her mid to late seventies who would ride her bicycle daily through our neighborhood dressed in a bikini. She was also very tanned, blond and her muscles were very toned. She attracted much attention as she rode around. She had her own fan club and they looked forward to her daily routine. I was very impressed by her and so was everyone else. I would run into her at the grocery store and she would always dress in figure hugging jeans and had all of the bag boys tripping over themselves to carry her groceries out to her car. It was a Cadillac Eldorado convertible of course. She even had a racy car too! She was living proof of my theory on aging. You could be very sexy and seventy at the same time.

Baby boomers are unique in that they are very interested in collecting things and nostalgia. They love the past and things they had when they were children, teenagers and young adults.

They love toy shows, antique fairs, classic car shows and there are hundreds of clubs where boomers meet to share these common interests.

No other generation has had as much enthusiasm as the baby boomers have with nostalgia and I am right there with them loving it too.

I find myself frequenting a restaurant in my area of Southwest Florida that is a real treat for old-fashioned toy lovers. Each table in this restaurant is a glass and wood showcase for toys from the turn of the century, 1920's, 30's, 40's, 50's and forward. There are tiny toys from cereal and Cracker Jack boxes, baseball cards, toy soldiers, dolls and all kinds of windup toys. There is also a large railroad train on tracks that is set up high by the ceiling area of the restaurant and it travels all around when the diners are enjoying their food. Patrons are encouraged to go into every room and to each floor of the building, to see the variety of toys and the pictures of movie starts of the past that line the walls.

I am overwhelmed by the variety and large numbers of nostalgic items in this restaurant and wonder how they collected all of them.

This restaurant is so popular and is always packed with people. If you look around, you will notice that most of them are baby boomer age. We love this kind of place which brings back memories of happy times when we were children and life was simpler, uncomplicated and we try to recapture this feeling by frequenting places like this restaurant. We like the warm and familiar feeling we get whenever we can reconnect with the past.

Our attitude toward reliving and preserving the past sets us apart and gives us comfort.

We can sometimes find ourselves dwelling on the negative aspects of growing older but I choose to think about the good things about aging and would like to remind you of those positive aspects such as:

1. I now have solutions for most problems and situations. I don't panic when difficulties arise. I have a wealth of resources in my mind that I call upon to solve problems and make decisions when needed. This is based on years of experience, trial and error and learning not to sweat the small stuff.

2. I no longer need to impress anyone anymore, like I felt I needed to when I was younger. I know who I am and actually like who I am, without needing the outward appearance of opulence, beauty and success. I celebrate the wonderful, creative, resourceful and strong individual I have become.

3. I get free checking accounts and discounts for travel, at the movies and in restaurants.

4. I don't have to prove anything anymore. I have already dared myself, did all of the scary things and survived.

5. I can give good advice to others because I have lived a lot and have experienced more than most younger people. I became the wise one, revered for my knowledge.

6. I am smart enough and secure enough to wear comfortable shoes and clothing. I remember, in my youth, having to lay down on the bed to be able to zip up my jeans and I wore platform shoes so high I would fall off of them and have trouble getting back up.

7. I no longer have to make excuses for what I do or how I live my life to anyone. I can now live for myself and don't care too much what other people think. I am true to the person I have become.

8. I am not intimidated or nervous about going to a party. I don't agonize over what I will wear or change my outfit three times before leaving the house. I pretty much know what looks good on me and how to put myself together nicely. I now have confidence in myself. It is no longer about being the most popular and most attractive in the room. I know how to work what I have and go to enjoy myself, instead of worrying about how I look and who will notice me.

9. I am somewhat financially secure. At this point in life I am not worrying about how I will pay the rent. I have already learned the hard way how to budget and live within my means.

10. I make better, more informed decisions. I have learned through success and failure what works best for me. I am not ruled by impulse but take more sensible, calculated risks.

11. I can act silly and no longer be embarrassed or care what others think. I remember how mortified I was when I was young and would fall down or be teased for being different. At this age, I can laugh it off and never give it a second thought.

12. I no longer have the pressure of youth. Finding a mate, getting married, raising children and having to succeed at all costs. This has already been done or I no longer see it as necessary to be happy in life. I can relax now and enjoy myself. Less responsibility is good.

13. I have my own AARP Magazine and group of lobbyists that look out for my interests. I have social security to look forward to. The younger generation may be on their own with only private investment accounts for their future.

Baby boomers attitudes have yet another uniqueness because they were exposed to more than one war during the course of their lives. They were actually the product of a war, World War II. The returning soldiers came home following the war and renewed their relationships with their wives and many births resulted from these reunions.

A central theme of boomers lives was war. We heard all about World War II from our parents who depicted stories about soldiers sent overseas to battle, wives that stayed behind taking on new roles, manning the jobs that men left and creating the products for the war.

Our mothers told us about the hardships of war, raising families alone and rationing of goods and services due to shortages from lower production and resources directed solely to the war effort instead of to the homeland.

The idea of women running families and working outside the home produced a whole new role model for our generation. We saw what women had achieved through necessity and it inspired us to take our roles even further into the workplace. We saw that women could have options in their lives and we reinvented the role of women from stay at home caretakers to career orientated executives.

This legacy of war caused our generation to appreciate life more than anyone. We not only lived through hearing about World War II but also the Korean War, Vietnam War, Gulf War and the War in Iraq. No other generation has experienced so much wartime. Our lives and attitudes had seriousness and urgency because of the effect of multiple wars.

I remember doing exercises in grade school where we would prepare ourselves for attack during the Cold War Era when Russia was arming itself with nuclear weapons and the threat of an attack was a possibility.

We were told by our teachers to put our heads under the tops of our desks and fold our hands over them. Sometimes we would be asked to leave our classrooms and go into the school's hallways, sit on the floor against the lockers and put our heads down. We were instructed to put our hands over our heads for protection in the event of a bomb threat.

You can imagine the impact this has on a small child. This somehow changes you and you have a sense of lost innocence that carries throughout your life.

This gives us the feeling that we need to live our lives to the fullest because we could cease to exist in a moment if a nuclear attack happened. We learned to want it all and want it now. We wanted to experiment with drugs, alternative styles of living. We questioned everything and became hippies and radical thinkers.

There is some good and bad to all of this and it created a generation that produced so many new ideas, change, innovation and modern technology. Our generation produced the first computer that revolutionized our way of living and brought with it a worldwide communication network that changed the way we live dramatically.

The dynamic nature of our attitudes is why we are the generation that can change the negativity and set the mark for positive aging.

2

HEALTH

Just because we are middle aged doesn't mean we have to give up and lose our figures. Don't ever buy into that theory. There is no reason at fifty you can't have as good a shape as you had at twenty. It is not that easy, but you don't have to slow down just because you are older. Your body will not rebel unless you let it.

Exercise should become as important to you as eating, drinking and breathing. It should be a priority. You wouldn't go to sleep without brushing your teeth and you shouldn't go to sleep without exercising either. Keeping your body in great condition will pay off positively. It will improve your mood and give you the energy to enjoy your life, raising your self-esteem and sense of self-worth.

A diet low in fat and with emphasis on fresh vegetables, fruit and whole grains has been proven to both extend and enhance your life and performance levels. We come from ancestors who were hunter-gatherers. Think of eating what whole foods one might find growing naturally and living in the natural environment.

Use the hunter-gatherer mentality as you approach your diet. Things that grow in the earth such as vegetables, fruits, rice, grains, nuts, soybeans and protein from what you could hunt, such as meat and fish. This would seem to be the best fuel for our bodies.

The less processing involved in the final product, the better. What is processing? Processing is how many changes the food has to go through from its original form and how many additives were put into it. The meat was not just cut and cooked, which would be the best way, but was ground up, cooked, salted, reformed and preservatives were added to it, the less desirable way, such as canned meats or deli style luncheon meats.

The same would be true for vegetables. Fresh picked, raw or cooked is best. Fresh, frozen would be second best. Vegetables in the can may be more convenient, but they usually include large amounts of salt, preservatives, coloring and other additives.

We live these fast-paced lifestyles where we need everything in an instant, pre-packaged, pre-cooked and easy to prepare. We have lost the great art and creativity of cooking a meal from scratch and making it an event. We have forgotten the benefits of fresh, home-cooked meals. We wonder how our grandmothers ate lard everyday and still lived to be ninety-three years old. This was way before our fat-free, sugar-free food obsessions of today.

It is a possibility, though not actually proven, that my grandmother survived well into her 90's because she lived on a farm, grew her own vegetables and raised the beef, pork and chicken she ate. All of it was fresh and unprocessed food, not pumped up with hormones and antibiotics. This may have made all of the difference in her health and longevity.

We need to simplify our eating habits and get down to basics. It is not that difficult to buy some fresh vegetables and place them in the microwave oven for a few minutes with a small amount of water for a wonderful, natural tasting side dish or snack. Even better yet, take a pot and use a vegetable steamer, put some water in the pot, then the vegetable steamer and place the vegetables on top of the steamer. Boil the water slowly for a few minutes until the vegetables are soft.

Instead of snacking on salty, greasy processed products such as potato and corn chips, how about eating nuts, seeds, dried fruits and whole grain crackers or biscuits. Pack them in small plastic bags or containers for convenience and carry them in your pocket or purse and keep them in your desk at work. One caveat is to be careful with nuts. Some people have severe allergic reactions to peanuts and other nuts and should avoid them. Also, remember to chew them up well and drink plenty of water with them.

Wean yourself off of sugar, bleached flour and saturated, hydrogenated fats. It is so easy to develop the habit of always looking for something sweet to eat. Our bodies are not meant to process excessive amounts of refined sugars but we continue to eat them more than we should. We reward ourselves with sweets, drown our sorrows with a pint of ice cream and have cravings for sugar-laden soft drinks. Do you know that there are *10 teaspoons* of sugar in *8 ounces* of most soft drink products? You wouldn't put ten teaspoons of sugar in your mouth, but you will gladly drink a can of cola and think nothing of it!

Cookies, cakes pies and ice cream are all right for occasional treats, unless your doctor has you on a strict diet, but everyday use can really damage your system. When we eat these sugary foods, our pancreas secretes a surge of insulin into our bodies. Excessive insulin causes a strain on our hearts, especially if we eat these things right before bedtime. Over time this can have a very adverse effect on the body. Try fresh fruit instead when you get a sweet tooth. I like blueberries, apples, raspberries and melons. They are so wonderful to eat and good for you too.

Try this experiment. Make a fist with your hand. This is approximately the size of your stomach. This size is what you should base your meal portion on instead of wolfing down the large portions we Americans have become accustomed to especially when eating out at restaurants and fast food establishments. The size of your fist is not really that large! We stuff our poor stomachs with two to four times its size with food when we eat, distending it to its limits and then wonder why we get a stomach ache or acid indigestion! We are not meant to eat the volume of food we put into our bodies. Making smaller portions is the easiest thing you can do to lose weight and improve your health. You wouldn't overfill your car's gas tank so why overfill your body? We're smarter than that and yet we continue to make this mistake over and over again ruining our health and feeling disgusted about our appearance. It also sends us to the doctor, seeking relief for acid indigestion, acid reflux, headaches and other ailments that we purposely bring upon ourselves.

Think of your body as you would a fast running sports car with a shiny new engine. When you are young, all of the parts are clean, run well and operate smoothly as long as you are in good health. As we age, the condition of your engine may be affected by what you put into it.

For your engine to run best, over the long haul, you wouldn't want to gum it up with heavy oil or sludge. This would slow it down and keep it from running at peak performance. You wouldn't put anything sticky or greasy into the gas tank because this could shut the engine down completely.

Yet we continue to put fat laden, sugary, heavily processed food into our bodies and then wonder why they don't work very well and, over time, completely break down.

This is a simplified example and we know our bodies aren't sports cars, but if you use this analogy, it may help you take better care of it.

If you are careful to use the best high performance motor oil and gasoline in your sports car and take it in for regular checkups, tune-ups and other maintenance, it should run well for many years. If you don't, it could have starting problems, trouble running efficiently and be ready for the junkyard far sooner than expected.

If we treat our bodies well by eating low fat, nutritious food and clean water, they should run more efficiently and last longer.

Think about this the next time you are tempted to eat or drink something that you know may not be good for you. It may help you resist the temptation.

In the European countries they serve much smaller portions than we do in America. In France, you only get a few tablespoons of each entree. You eat slower and savor each fork full noticing the aroma, texture and flavors from your food instead of just wolfing it down. The French food can be very rich, but because they eat smaller portions, they don't seem to have the weight problems we Americans do. Dinnertime to them is an event to be enjoyed for hours in a relaxed environment. Presentation of the food is very important too. They take the time to include fancy garnish that is both beautiful and edible too.

In our hustle-bustle world, we don't take the time to really make our dinner an event that is relaxed and enjoyable. Many times it is just a race to see how fast we can get finished and on to other activities, or we eat sitting in front of the television set. We are in such a rush, we sometimes don't even bother to taste our food. We don't take the time to enjoy the meal, relax, savor the flavors and take pleasure in it as a very important part of our day. We need to ask ourselves why we are in such a hurry. This is certainly not good for our health or our need to de-stress ourselves at the end of the day.

We also get into bad habits of eating on the run when we are away from home. We grab a burger, fries and a cola from a fast food establishment to satisfy our hunger. The burger and fries are loaded with fat, the bun has too many carbohydrates and is made from white flour and sugar and the cola has over ten teaspoons of sugar in every eight ounces. Instead, we should take the time in the morning to pack foods we can munch on during the day. Cut up vegetables, fruit, nuts, raisins and take some bottled water with you. Many of these items already come pre-packaged for convenience so you don't have any excuses for not taking the time to make better food selections. This would be much better for your health and make you feel better too.

Of course everyone should consult their physician before radically changing their diet or exercise routine. This is important. It is also important to follow the directions of your doctor regarding any health conditions that need medical attention.

Americans are more overweight today than ever and I feel that this is because we have become so accustomed to large portions. Serving sizes are so large. We don't need to eat the volume of food we eat. People think they are getting more for their money when they eat out if they get larger portions, but it is killing them.

Whenever I want to lose a few pounds, I cut my portions in half, eat only half of what is on my plate and put the remaining half of the food in the refrigerator where I can eat more in case I can't hold out until the next meal. When I can't hold out, I just eat a little of what is left. By doing this, you eat less without feeling so deprived. Your stomach gets used to less food and after a while you don't even need to go into that other half in the refrigerator. The original half that you eat is filling enough.

It is a good idea to pay attention to the time during your meals when you become full instead of just wolfing down your food and later having that uncomfortable feeling you get when you eat too much.

Don't give up your favorite foods. Eat less of them. Combine them with good foods and you won't have as much room in your stomach for them.

If you love potato chips, eat them, but eat less of them. Take a bowl and put a few potato chips, some almonds, walnuts and a few raisins in it. Eat this instead of just sitting there with the entire bag of chips in front of you.

Really taste the potato chips and don't just shove them into your mouth. Savor the crunch, the saltiness, the rich, flavorful essence. Take a long time to chew them and concentrate on eating instead of something else. Really enjoy the experience of eating.

Buy potato chips with just a few ingredients such as potatoes, canola oil, salt. Don't buy ones that have chemicals, preservatives or anything you cannot pronounce. Simple whole foods are the best.

Recently I have become more aware of the growth hormones, antibiotics and pesticides in our meat and dairy products. I have decided to purchase more organic fruits, vegetables, meat, milk, butter, nuts and other foods that do not contain these additives.

After eating these unadulterated foods, a remarkable thing happened to me. Where I once had gray hair, I now had dark brown roots growing. My skin glowed more than ever and actually had a wonderful sheen to it!

I also am becoming more aware of the chemicals in our shampoo, toothpaste and soap. Many of these products contain chemicals such as sodium laurel sulfate, propylene glycol and other petroleum based additives that can be hazardous to our health. I researched this on the internet and found some serious warnings.

I now purchase products at my neighborhood health food store that contain natural ingredients.

The shampoos seem to make my hair thicker and the conditioners with natural oils make my hair very shiny and healthier looking. This is just my opinion and you should just try it and see if it works for you.

I quit using deodorant bar soap to shower and now use a natural bar soap made with goat's milk. It smells just wonderful and leaves my skin soft and healthy looking.

These items are more expensive but to me, they are worth the price because I feel better using them and the results are amazing.

More and more I am also moving to a vegetarian diet. A number of my friends and co-workers were getting cancer and I was very concerned about getting it myself. I noticed that when one co-worker got prostrate cancer, his doctor told him to eliminate all meat from his diet. I did some research on the Internet under the cancerproject.com website and read about what type of diet would help ward off cancer.

Time and again I would see that the articles stressed lots of fruit, vegetables, grains and a vegetarian diet without meat or dairy products. I wondered why no meat or dairy, eggs or any animal products. Why do doctors wait until we get cancer to suggest dietary changes? Why shouldn't everyone have this information before they get cancer?

I am very glad I became interested in this subject because, in doing some research, I found that I could help prevent this serious disease.

By adopting a low fat, vegetarian diet with fruit, vegetables, whole grains and legumes, I would be helping my body fight off the cancer cell reproduction that gets out of control and causes tumors and cell abnormalities. Now there are no guarantees and this type of diet is very hard to stick with, but I figure that even if I do some of it, it will help me stay healthier.

I do not condone any specific diet, but I encourage you to do some research and see what works for you.

We are exposed to many chemicals in the foods we eat and the products we use. Many of them can be harmful and I feel that the less we are exposed to, the better for our overall health.

It is your responsibility to read the ingredients on the labels of the food you eat and the products you use and if you see names you do not recognize, research them and find out if there is any reliable information on whether they are harmful of pose a risk to your health.

You can go overboard worrying about this subject and like I said previously you need to be practical and reasonable both doing your own research and with the assistance of your doctor, find what is best for you.

Food is such a big part of our lives and we don't want to become too obsessive about it. Eating should be enjoyable and fun and we should not burden ourselves with worrying too much about it, but enjoy it to the fullest!

We eat because we are hungry and our body physically needs food, but we also eat to relieve stress and to fill emotional needs that should be filled by something else.

Stress eating is a real problem. I believe this is an important factor in the growing obesity situation in our country. I catch myself doing this, especially at work. We have created lives that are so fast-paced, full of responsibilities. We put pressure on ourselves to create success at the highest level financially and with our careers. Many times we cannot keep up with it all and this causes us stress.

Why do we take on so much and why are we always in such a hurry? Why do we burden ourselves with so much debt, work and other demands? Aren't we good enough just as we are?

Society puts a great deal of pressure on us to achieve lofty goals, lavish lifestyles, work at high-powered jobs and raise children all at the same time. We have become super women and super men but at what cost to our health and family life.

With this in mind, it isn't any wonder that we overeat to relieve the stress. Food comforts us; it is reliable, doesn't let us down and is always there when we need it. It is legal, can be purchased anytime for little cost or effort. We don't have to go out and hunt for our food as our ancestors did. We don't have to grow our food, so we expend little calories obtaining our food, which could explain why our ancestors did not have the obesity problems we see in our country today.

Love yourself enough to take the best possible care of your health. Sometimes people will not buy the fresh fruit and vegetables because they said it is too expensive, but consider this, you are saving yourself $100,000 that the heart bypass operation may cost you in the future!!!! It's not so expensive anymore is it?

It seems to me that people overeat to fill a hole left empty because of lack of love, attention, people contact and purposeful living. We turn to food instead of others to bring us comfort. It is readily available, reliable, loyal, trustworthy and always there when we need it. These are things that we don't seem to find in the people we know as often as we find it in the food we eat.

We live isolated lives in many ways and fear reaching out because we may be rejected. This isolation contributes to our sedentary lifestyle and overeating patterns. When you become more social you get out and away from that television set and snack food habits.

If you live a purposeful life with rich, loving and faithful relationships, you will find that you eat less. When you are hugged, loved, nurtured and praised, you don't need that extra food for comfort. You get comfort from your daily life. If you don't have a close family or friend, try doing some volunteer work at a hospital, senior home or daycare center. This will bring you joy, purpose and many new relationships. Believe me, those that you serve will appreciate you and look forward to your visits. If you do this you will also have less time to eat.

Think about when you first fall in love with someone. There is a lot of physical attention, cuddling, kissing and holding each other. You are so excited just to see that other person and it energizes you. You find that you usually lose weight because you are concentrating on what you have, this beautiful relationship with this other person, instead of filling a hole because you do not have this in your life. The love relationship and all it brings to you fills this hole.

Try this experiment. Carry around a 10-pound weight while you go about your daily tasks. It becomes very difficult after awhile. Think of this as the extra 10 or 20 pounds that you are overweight and just realize what it is doing to your body. It puts a heavy amount of stress and strain on your limbs and it just plain wears you out!

When you are even more than 10 or 20 pounds overweight you are even more tired and your body can only take so much before it starts giving you problems. Your bones start to ache, you get indigestion, dizziness, shortness of breath and your whole quality of life diminishes.

It is very difficult to take charge of your health and weight but just taking small steps to start a program is so beneficial. You have to just decide that your life and you are important and worth more than anything else. You deserve to be at the best possible physical shape that you can be.

By taking steps to improve your health and fitness, you can begin the road to an improved sense of self-worth and more energy and happiness than you can imagine. Your attitude toward this endeavor is so important. Think healthy thoughts and you will be healthy! This may sound unbelievable to you but it does actually work.

I recall hearing stories about cancer patients using mental imagery to command their bodies to heal themselves. They would practice a kind of meditation. They would lie down and completely relax and visually imagine seeing their good cells attacking their cancerous cells.

I had a supervisor who I worked for many years ago who was plagued by migraine headaches. One day I went into his office to discuss a work problem with him and found him sitting in a chair in a deep trance. He noticed me as I broke his concentration and told me that he could concentrate and wish his headaches away. He said that he very seldom relied on medication for his pain and I found this both unbelievable and very fascinating.

I believe that the mind is a powerful tool in dealing with our health. If we get up in the morning thinking we are going to be sick, we can work ourselves into feeling tired, nauseous, have headaches and even develop sniffles, diarrhea and other flu-like symptoms when we aren't actually sick at all. Over time this can become chronic and lead to serious actual illness.

Do you let a little headache or sniffle become overwhelming making you take to your bed or do you just shrug it off and go on about your business, take a couple of aspirin and not let it ruin your day? Your attitude toward pain or illness can really make a difference in your health.

I was always afraid of getting fired from my job if I took a sick day off so I would do what I needed to do to get through the day. I was raising a child as a single mother and just the thought of losing my job motivated me beyond belief. For many years I would get chronic sinus headaches and certain times of the year I would get them more frequently. I couldn't afford the days off of work, so I would just force myself to get up, take a few sinus pills and other pain killers and go off to work. I found that after a while my headache would lessen as I got my mind off of it by being busy at work. I also found that just the act of moving about doing my daily activities helped get my body going. It seemed to make the medication work faster and allow my body to heal itself.

Even exercise made my headaches go away faster. It was very difficult but I would just get outside in the fresh air and start walking for about ten minutes and then run. After about a forty-five minute walk, run session, the headache would be gone. This amazed me the first few times I tried it. It reinforced the powerful effect exercise has on the body. It gets your blood flowing and more oxygen gets into your lungs and this helps alleviate the pain. At times I would try to go without taking any medication and just try exercise alone and many times this was all I needed.

Exercise also gets your mind off of the pain by placing your concentration elsewhere, on the beauty of the great outdoors and on the activity itself. You feel more alive in nature and revived.

I believe our bodies are miracles of nature and designed to take care of themselves. We may just need to learn to use them to heal what minor ailments may come our way. Tap into the energy and properties already right at our disposal.

Remember, you are responsible for your weight and your health. Educate yourself about health and fitness and never stop learning because new developments are made in these fields on a daily basis. Learn all you can about preventing disease so your later years can be both healthful and you may extend your longevity too.

3

EXERCISE

I can't say enough about exercise and the benefits it provides mentally, physically and spiritually. I have been exercising all of my life. My first form of exercise was playing as a child. I loved to roller skate, ride my bicycle, climb trees, run, ice skate, walk in the woods, swim and go fishing. What great fun!

At the time, I didn't know that what I was doing was good for me. All I knew was that it was fun, made me feel good and I slept like a baby!

This is how I would like you to approach exercise. Like a child, find something that is fun to do and gives you a good workout too. All of the things I did as a child were forms of exercise. You can approach your exercise routine as drudgery or as the most fun of the day. It's all up to you.

Exercise is like brushing your teeth. You must do it everyday to thrive. Always check with your doctor before you plan an exercise program. Work with them to assist you with the forms that will work best for you and your health. Dr. Wayne Dyer in his motivation tapes, <u>How to be a No Limit Person</u>, made this statement, "If you don't take the time for exercise now, you will have to take the time for illness later."

Set aside a regular time each day for exercise just like you set aside time for eating, sleeping, brushing your teeth and bathing. It is so important that you need to look at it as a necessary part of your regular day. I know I mention this many times in this chapter, but your longevity may depend on it. Keeping this in mind you will stick to it just like you do the other things in your regular daily schedule. Believe me, the payoff is tremendous.

I run, ride my bicycle, walk and work out at the gym where I live. One of the things I looked for when I purchased a home was whether there was a convenient gym nearby where I could work out. I need some place that is close by to keep me going regularly. I find that if I have to get in my car and drive somewhere, I lose my motivation. I also picked a community that has many sidewalks and beautiful landscaping so I can get outside and run and walk anytime I wish and it also has the benefit of relaxing me just looking at the lush surroundings. This is so important to me to have these amenities right where I live and because of this I use them daily.

When I go out on my bicycle, it is the best part of my day. How wonderful to ride in the open air and just take in all the beautiful scenery. It both improves my health and lifts my spirits, while relieving stress and giving me tranquility. My body starts producing chemicals that make me feel wonderful.

Always keep in mind safety when you go riding. Get a bicycle that feels comfortable and fits your needs. The ones that make you sit upright seem to work the best for me. They even have recreational bicycles now that you can sit on the seat and still have your feet touch the ground. They remind me of the bikes we rode as kids, with the wider tires and larger seats. They are so comfortable and safe that even if you are a little fearful of riding, you need not worry.

Always wear a helmet made for riding and keep alert to traffic from vehicles and pedestrians. Make sure your bicycle is equipped with a good headlight and a red rear flashing light for riding at night. This is so important for safety and sometimes your daytime ride extends longer than you had planned. Riding in the darkness can make it difficult to see obstructions in the roadway and drivers in vehicles may not be able to see you. Keep in mind your safety and you will find the most enjoyable fun ever.

I love bicycle riding so much, I never want my rides to end. I always feel a little sad putting my bicycle away at the end of the ride. It must be a throwback to my childhood when I never wanted to come back into the house after playtime was over.

In the community I live in, I see groups of people on their bicycles in the early morning getting together to ride. They are usually smiling as they go about their exercise which can be so much fun. It reminds me of when we were little kids and we all got together on our bikes for the day's adventure.

Another form of exercise I like to do is running. I do not recommend this for everyone. If you are already a runner, you can do this form of exercise, but if you are not, consult your physician before doing this form of exercise. You can benefit almost as much from brisk walking and it is less jarring on the body.

If you choose to run, start off slowly. When I first started running, many years ago, I alternated walking and running. I would warm up with some regular walking, then walk briskly for about ten minutes and then run for about five minutes. Experiment with this to see what is most comfortable to you. You don't need to overdo it in order to benefit from it. Remember to keep it enjoyable. That is the key to keeping it a regular part of your routine. We have a tendency to keep doing the things we enjoy and give up on the things we don't.

As you progress with your routine, you will find yourself running more and walking less. This takes time however, so be patient and do it at a comfortable pace and don't overdo your workout. It doesn't pay off to push yourself beyond your comfort zone.

A big part of a running program is good shoes. I cannot say enough about this. The first time I purchased a good pair of running shoes, I could not believe the difference it made in my routine. I felt like I had clouds on my feet! I had spring to my step and my knees, shins and ankles felt so much better with the extra cushioning the quality shoes provided. My first good pair were from the Nike Air product line and cost over $100.00. This was over ten years ago and at the time I agonized over spending so much because it was a large sum of money for someone in my pay level. It was a big stretch for me to spend this at the time, but it was so worth it. This extra cushioning saves both your knees and hips and makes you want to work out because it is so much more comfortable. Running can put a strain on many parts of your body. It is a good idea to be very careful to not overdue it when it comes to this form of exercise.

One great benefit from running is that it really streamlines your body shape. Your hips get narrower and your legs get very toned. This is also a wonderful way to lose weight and these results are true motivators.

I also like to take long walks. Usually I enjoy picking up the pace and doing a brisk walk but sometimes I just like to take it slow and really take in and enjoy the scenery, smells and just the pure joy of being alive and able to enjoy nature. Walking can be almost as effective as running when done correctly as a form of exercise. It is safe and less taxing to the body than running.

As I mentioned above for running it is a good idea to get a well-made pair of walking shoes and make this form of exercise an important part of your lifestyle. I like Rockport and Easy Spirit walking shoes.

Find a scenic place to walk and vary your locations and routines to keep things interesting. Use a quick pace after you warm up by starting slowly and swing your arms back and forth for additional aerobic benefits. Even if the weather is cold, bundle up with layers of clothing and get outdoors or you can use your local mall as a walking place. It will do your body and spirit good and give you a feeling of well-being that is well worth the effort.

Many people where I live in South Florida enjoy golfing. It gets you outside and makes you move. Some people prefer to walk the golf course and others prefer to use a golf cart. Golfing exercises your upper body area by utilizing your shoulders, arms, wrists, hands, head and neck muscles. It also exercises your lower body with the walking and bending part of the game.

The game of golf also can be very frustrating. This will exercise your feet and legs when you stamp the ground after a bad shot and make fists with your hands while raising your arms in anger! On the other hand, if you are having a good game, the same applies. You will be raising your arms in happiness and jumping up and down with joy at that perfect putt.

Even when I am traveling out of town, as I do occasionally for my job, I find ways to exercise. Most hotels have workout rooms with treadmills, stationary bikes, step machines and free weights. They also have swimming pools that are so very relaxing. I love going in the pool and doing laps, leg kicks and just floating along enjoying the cool, crisp water that refreshes my whole body.

Don't worry about having to put on a swimsuit. Bodies come in all shapes and sizes, so learn to love yours. Just remember to appreciate it instead of hating it. Your body takes you wherever you want to go and is always there when you need it.

I even find places to take enjoyable walks and runs when I am out of town. You can usually find a park, zoo or nice neighborhood to get your exercise.

I have a friend in California that I go to visit occasionally. He lives in a very beautiful neighborhood. I take long walks there and look at the homes that are all so different and some have wonderful gardens with colorful flowers and plants.

Some of the houses have even been used in movies and on television shows. One time I was visiting, there were large semi-tractor trailer trucks, cameras and actors recording a television show in front of a large, white house. How exciting this was for me as I went about my walk to see this action going on while I was enjoying my exercise.

There are other easy things you can do for exercise that have been around for years. Using a jump rope can be both fun and will give you a good overall workout. Try a Hula Hoop for waist exercising.

My son loves to play catch with a baseball when he comes to visit me. It is a fun way to get some exercise and the time flies by. Before you know it you have been exercising for an hour and don't even realize it because it is so much fun. Look out for the ball though. It took some bruises before I learned how to dodge it.

Just remember, exercise can be fun and the payoffs are tremendous to your health, spirit, happiness and sense of self-esteem.

4

SUCCESS

What is success really? It can be defined in many ways. Some people define it in monetary values. If a person makes a great deal of money, to the outside world, they are successful. Others define success as finding work you love. Success can also be found in someone raising a happy and healthy family.

Does success end when youth is lost? I don't think so. As we get older, we still can seek out and find avenues of success. After we have lived a number of years in our life we can better evaluate what skills and talents we have and just know what it is that we are really good at doing.

I realized somewhere in my mid-forties that what I am really good at is business and putting resources and people together to get projects done. I can find good solutions to problems. I am an action-orientated person who is not afraid to make the hard decisions and follow through to get the job done. I also have strong powers of persuasion and can motivate people. I didn't have these skills and confidence in my youth. It took a long time to develop, learn and practice while actually working in business on actual projects to gain the necessary skills that now come easy as a result of this hard work.

You too can take an inventory of your skills and find new and exciting areas to consider as choices for careers or as a business of your own. Many people, by the time they are fifty years of age or older, have a retirement income and can pursue opportunities without worries about how much money it will pay. Those that do need that steady income can find it too.

Just ask yourself what is it that you really enjoy. What would you do happily even if you didn't receive any pay? What type of work would you be excited to get up each morning and go out to do with a great big smile on your face? Finding out what that is may not be very easy. Maybe you love to go out in the garden and will work for hours planting flowers, arranging bushes and shrubs, trees and just being out in the natural environment. Do you know that you could do this for others as a business? With the hectic lives most people live, they don't have time for this type of work and you could build them a perfectly wonderful garden, make them happy and get paid doing what you love. This is just one example. There are many others.

I love animals and have often wondered what it would be like to have a business where I could enjoy the animals and still make money. A petting zoo or nature center might be fine and provide enjoyment for others. There would be a good quantity of work involved in this kind of project, but I know that I could make it fun. Just being around animals makes me smile and want to just go and hug all of them. This kind of job is what you should look for when choosing your life's work.

I remember going to a place just like the one I mentioned above when I was a child. It was in a suburban area, outside of Chicago, and it was called Trailside. It was an animal sanctuary and people would bring pets they no longer wanted and they would be cared for and given a good home here. I remember seeing all species of animals there from frogs to raccoons, dogs, cats, snakes, ducks and other interesting animals. I always looked forward to going there and remembered the people who worked, in this fun environment, were very dedicated to taking care of the animals entrusted to them. We even brought our pet dachshund, Fritz, to Trailside when he was older and had trouble getting around. He had aged and gained too much weight. He had trouble getting around on his little legs and needed help. The proprietor of the sanctuary took him under her wing and made him her personal pet. She spoiled him rotten and built a monument to him after he died.

Finding your true calling can give you a new lease on life bringing you renewed positive energy and raising your confidence that can be lost as we get older. The positive feedback you get from those that you serve in whatever career path you decide to take, can really make a difference in your life.

So take a few minutes to contemplate your future and give it a try. Even if you just do it part-time to see how it works. Don't give up your regular job until you see that it is what you want and can pay the bills. This way you won't have to be afraid of taking this new risk. Good luck and start thinking about how you can find your dream job.

5

RELATIONSHIPS

I am a veteran of the dating and relationship game. I have been divorced for over 28 years and during this time I have had a few relatively long term relationships, periods of being completely alone and times when I was just enjoying dating and being with friends in groups, instead of one on one relationships.

Each chapter in the adventures of the man/woman dynamic challenges and educates and can bring both ultimate joy and unbearable sorrow.

We grow up in a culture that teaches women that from the time they are very young, their ultimate goal is to marry and have a family. Society puts a lot of pressure on women to the point that they feel like complete failures if they don't accomplish this goal. I gave into this pressure and spent a great deal of time and energy trying to find Mr. Right. Unfortunately, in the beginning, I made many wrong choices. I fell for the good-looking, tough guys instead of looking for a kind, stable and successful, goal-orientated man. It seems like some girls are smarter when it comes to picking men. They know exactly what they want and they go after it. I, on the other hand, had such low self-esteem that I settled for boyfriends that were not right for me or did not treat me well, just to have someone around. It didn't matter. I just wanted to have a boyfriend.

I tolerated bad behavior, alcoholism, drug abuse, physical and mental abuse and unfaithfulness all in the name of love.

I was very naïve as a young woman. I didn't know how to recognize an alcoholic or drug abuser. I grew up around this behavior and thought it was acceptable. My father drank often and I didn't think much about it. I had relationships with alcoholics that proved to be very damaging to me. The men were good, decent people, but the alcohol and drugs made them irresponsible, abusive, unpredictable, unreliable and a financial burden. Life is difficult and complicated enough. When you add all of the difficulties the overuse of alcohol and drug abuse brings, it becomes unbearable.

Look for the signs of alcoholism and drug use and avoid relationships with others that have problems with either. Groups like Al-Anon and organizations like the Partnership for a Drug-Free America provide wonderful literature and resources for identifying addiction problems in others.

Some people like this kind of drama in their lives and actually court it, thinking it is exciting, but believe me this can only lead to much heartbreak and pain and even abuse and death.

Seek a partner that brings you a sense of security, calmness, serenity and happiness. Laugh together and have fun. Find that special person that is happy, compliments you, thinks the world of you and lets you know it. If they don't, they are not *worthy* of you. Learn to be self-sufficient and independent enough to be able to say no and walk away from those individuals that put you down, lower your self-esteem, are not supportive of your goals and dreams, feel threatened by your success or happiness and don't want the very best for you.

You are *better off alone* than compromising on this just because you think you are incomplete without another person in your life. Your life is too short and precious to waste living with a toxic person who brings you down.

Place the emphasis on pursuing your own dreams and goals and in doing this you will attract the right kind of mate, one that is doing the same as you are, pursuing their own dreams and goals. You will then compliment each other with mutual support mentally, spiritually and without the desperate dependency needs that characterize those people that have not realized their own potential prior to entering into relationships with others who are controlling, negative, abusive, dangerous forces that rob you of the wonderful and fantastic life you deserve and strive to live.

Don't look around for someone to take you away from all of this or take on the responsibility for living your life. Instead become your own *knight in shining armor*.

When I was growing up I read the stories about how the knight in shining armor came and rescued the fair maiden and raised her from obscurity and drudgery and brought her into a life of luxury and happiness. For many years of my life I believed that this would happen and actually put my life on hold and waited for this knight to come along.

Boy was I in for a reality check! I actually went about looking for the knight and made mistake after mistake choosing to devote all of my time and energy into relationships instead of developing my own skills and talents and making my own life the best it could be.

At some point I got the message after realizing that the knight in shining armor was a fairy tale and that it wasn't fair to expect the man to create a life for me. I needed to do that myself. I needed to be my own knight in shining armor and take charge and the responsibility to make my life into something special and meaningful. The knight could share it with me but should not be responsible for directing it. That was my job and I finally took it seriously.

You need to do the same with your life. You are responsible for making it what you want it to be. Don't delegate that to anyone else. Don't ever give that kind of control away to some other person. You will never realize your true potential or feel whole as a person if you give this power away. Do not give the responsibility for your own life to someone else. It is not romantic and at some point you will resent them and yourself for not striving to be all that you can be in your own right.

For some reason women are fascinated by this knight in shining armor story with the man coming to rescue them and make them complete. We are complete entities by ourselves. Knowing this gives us the power rather than letting someone else take it from us. Many of us buy into the knight theory and it keeps us from fulfilling our own destiny and achieving our own goals.

It is easy to give the responsibility for creating a life for yourself to another person but what may be easy today could become a nightmare later on. You could wake up one day living a life you never wanted and feel trapped and miserable wondering how you ever got there. Worse yet, since you do not have the power or skills to make it on your own, you could be facing an abusive knight who tries to control you and keep you locked up in his castle forbidding you to ever escape.

Relegating the power in your life to someone else can leave you helpless and hopeless. This alone should inspire you to develop yourself and become a whole person before you go out and seek the person you want to share your life with. You will be a better partner and put less demands on them. This is the way a partnership should work.

I recently saw a clip of a famous movie star on television jumping up and down gleefully announcing that he was so very much in love. Why is it that being in love gives us so much hope, happiness and excitement? Shouldn't we feel that way everyday of our life whether we are in the throws of a new love or not? Why is it that falling in love is so euphoric? Can life be euphoric without falling in love?

I have thought about this often. Who decided that we all should desire to fall in love, marry and have children? Not everyone is cut out for this lifestyle and many try it over and over again and it doesn't work out for them. There is a reason this happens. We don't all fit into the mold. Many people feel trapped, suffocated and held back in this type of arrangement yet many still try to make it work because they feel that this is what they are *supposed* to do. They feel like there is something wrong with them if they don't marry and have a family.

I feel that we are put on this earth with the responsibility to live our best life whatever that may be. Whether married or single we need to fulfill our own hopes and dreams. We should not feel guilty or inadequate because we choose to remain single or maybe even never meet someone we feel we would want to marry. People have rushed into or forced relationships and marriage and later divorced because they were just trying to fit into a pre-ordained pattern of living that was set up by someone else who knew nothing about them. People spend years of their lives in unfulfilled marriages because they dread the idea of divorce and being on their own. They would rather be miserable and *safe* than be out there on their own facing uncertainty and loneliness.

I know a woman who has been married four times and is now engaged to her fifth partner. She marries and then somehow always needs other men in addition to her husband. She has numerous affairs and yet still wants to continue to get married. I don't know why she doesn't just stay single and date all of the different men she seems to need. What surprises me most though is that there are men out there that still want to marry her, even though she has a terrible track record when it comes to staying married. Granted, she is attractive, but you would think that the men would not want to marry a woman who cheats on them.

It takes courage to go out into the world and live a lifestyle outside of societal pressure to marry and have a family. A person is forced to become whole and fulfilled on their own if they choose not to marry. For many this works out better and it is nice to see that people are trying it and finding lives filled with success and happiness.

More and more we are seeing a variety of family styles such as women as heads of households, gay couples together raising children or not, single households with children or not, community living and it is becoming more acceptable and changing the face of the family ideal.

By all means do not feel short-changed or less of a person if you never marry or have children. Make your own choices and live your life the way you decide is best for you and you will find the greatest peace and happiness you can imagine.

If you are married or in a committed relationship do not take it for granted. This sounds trite and you have heard this a thousand times but remember that the fact that you found someone you think enough of to spend the rest of your life with is rare enough. Many people never find that special someone, that soul mate, a person you actually love unconditionally.

Both men and women lose interest over time in committed relationships unless they are determined to keep it interesting and alive. Partners can become complacent and take each other for granted. Sex becomes less frequent, arguments more frequent and many start looking elsewhere for new relationships because they think something is wrong with the one they are in presently.

This need not happen if you always remember to treat your partner the best way you possibly can and value them above anything else. Be generous with compliments and do it with sincerity. I cannot stress enough the power of complimenting your partner. It is one of the most neglected areas of relationships. *People need to know how you feel about them and that they are special.* Both women and men love to hear that they are beautiful, handsome, you love their dress, their tie, how they do their hair and how they make you feel. They need to know that you still find them sexy and that you appreciate what they do for you. Remember this and practice it each and every day of your life together.

Don't worry that this will make you sound corny or that you are a wus or a sissy because you do this. The smile on your partner's face is the true testimony to how effective supporting each other can be.

The most popular men and women know how to compliment people and people remember how you make them feel about themselves. If you make them feel wonderful and self-confident they will look forward to seeing you and spending time with you.

Relationships can end or die if they are not nurtured in this way. People think they can just neglect the other person and if they don't like it, they can just find another person to love, but this is not that easy. If you think this way you will just dive into another relationship that will result in this same kind of situation, one that loses interest. How many times are you willing to do this over and over again when you know in your heart it will result in the same heartbreaking ending?

We live in such a disposable society and relationships, many times, are treated like throw away garbage that are easily discarded when the going gets tough or problems arise. It is a sad commentary on our lives that this exists and over half of marriages end in divorce. We need to stop and take more time to select our life partner and stick with them.

Use some sensibility and develop and cherish the relationship you are in, if it is worth it to you. Don't make the mistake of jumping from one into another without giving it all you have to offer and really working to keep it special.

Each week mark your calendar to do something unexpected for your partner. Make them feel like *the greatest person in the world* and you will both benefit from the experience.

Hold them in your arms and look into their eyes and tell them that you are going to be there for them *no matter what happens* and really mean it.

Don't laugh, this is really important. Take it from someone who has really been neglected in relationships. I know and I am certain others can relate to this fact. I am not quite sure why this has happened to me but I think that most men feel that I am so self-sufficient that I don't need to hear this, but it is so untrue.

Don't presume that your partner knows how you feel. They need to know where they stand with you and often. Let them know that you love them, and how important they are to you. Security in a relationship is foremost and if you can't provide this to the person you are with you have no business being with them.

Having a partner is such a special gift and to make sure your relationship grows and lasts forever, you need to prize it like the greatest treasure you can imagine and never lose sight of this. Your partner will not live forever and your time together goes quickly. *Never take it for granted.*

If you are single, celebrate your life. Your duty is to go out into the world and live it to its fullest. That is my challenge to you and I want you to love every minute of it!

Whether you are married or in a committed relationship treat it like your most treasured possession. Either way, single or married you can have a fantastic life in your fifties and beyond.

6

LIVE YOUR DREAM

What is your dream? I have a few and it is so much fun to just dream away about these wonderful fantasies!

One dream I have is to have my own farm with about 20 or more acres, cows, horses, chickens, dogs, cats, ferrets, birds and grow my own food. I'd like it to have a small lake and a beautiful wooded area where I could take meditative and relaxing walks and just relate to all of the beautiful nature around me.

I dream about waking up each morning and going out for a long ride on my horse, milk the cows, collect the eggs and pick fresh fruit and vegetables from my garden. I see myself sitting on a fence, gazing out into my pasture, where cows and horses would be playing. I'm a farm girl at heart and this would be the ultimate life for me.

I know you have a dream too. Sit down and write it down on paper. Figure out what it would take to reach this goal and live this dream. It may seem far from your reach, but there is no reason you shouldn't be able to reach this goal and live your dream.

Start by making a list of what you will need to do to accomplish your dream. When you break things down into parts, it doesn't seem so impossible or unattainable. As you check off each task you will be on your way to accomplishing your dream life.

At first pick out the things you can accomplish right away. If you need money to help with your dream, write down ways you can get this money such as:

1. Take on a second part-time job.

2. Economize by brown bagging your lunch instead of eating out, shop the sales, make home made gifts instead of purchasing them, sell off items you no longer need or use.

If you need to return to school in order to live your dream, write down how you could do this, for example:

1. What school will I need to attend and how long?

2. How will I pay for the classes I attend?

3. How do I fit this into my current schedule?

You may also need help from others in order to live your dream. To find my farm, I would need to :

1. Find a good realtor.

2. Check the local newspapers listings for property for sale.

3. Look up land and farms for sale on the internet.

4. Have someone mentor you; find someone who has already done what you want to do and pick their brain; find out how they accomplished their dream and mimic it.

I can't say enough about how very important it is to get down to the business of seriously pursuing your dream life, whatever it is. Life is so short and many times people put off their dreams and get too busy just getting by and surviving. Their dreams get set aside and by the time they actually start thinking about it, it's too late to start. Therefore, it is crucial to a fulfilled life to figure this out now and act upon it.

Make a list of what your dream is for your life. Write down all of the things you will need to do to reach it and who can help you get there.

Another example, after I turned fifty, I got up one day and said to myself that I have always wanted to be able to sing. Many of you can relate to the idea of being a singer, performing in front of a crowd and receiving a standing ovation! What a rush that would be! How many times have you been in the shower or listening to the radio and you put that imaginary microphone in front of your mouth and make believe that you are a star. It's so much fun to imagine this and I wanted to try it.

I looked at the yellow pages of the telephone book and found a few schools in my area that offered lessons and I called them. I was surprised that they were so inexpensive, around $15.00 per half-hour. I was very frightened at the idea of going to the lessons and really doing poorly, so I practiced a song and sang it into a tape recorder to see just how awful it would be. Actually it sounded pretty good and it gave me the courage to proceed.

I found some learn to sing programs on the Internet with CD's and practice tapes to also help me develop my skills. In trying out different sounds and styles I decided that the old standards suited me the best and I proceeded to practice them. "Stormy Weather" was a favorite and I love to sing it. Usually I practice in my car so no one will have to listen to my less than perfect attempts at what you could call singing. I record myself on a tape recorder and this helps me improve my singing. Someday I would like to get enough songs recorded to put on a CD to give to my friends or maybe even sell. This is great fun and I feel so good when I get to do this.

What do you dream about the most? When you need to escape from the moment, where do you go and what are you doing? Think about this carefully.

I usually find myself at the beach, walking along the water. I also find myself on a farm with cows, horses and other animals living peacefully on acreage away from the business of our fast-paced environment.

I have heard the question, "What would you do if you knew you only had six months to live?" Where would you go and what would you be doing? What haven't you done that you have always wanted to do? Who do you want to spend more time with?

Answering these questions can be difficult for some people and easier for others, but we should examine our answers to gain insight into what we need to do to get to our dream without the pressure of only having a short time to live. It is easy to forget that we have a limited amount of time on earth and we need to make the most of it. We do not have time to waste living an unsatisfactory life and never doing anything about it. Why wait for the time in your life when you really only have six months to live. Why not figure it out and live your dream today.

I dated a man many years ago who struck me as being kind of an adventurer. He worked as a hairdresser, but had great dreams of someday buying a trimaran, a three-hulled catamaran, and sailing in and around the Virgin Islands doing diving salvage work. He told me that there were many shipwrecks under the water and that he could make a good living doing this type of work.

He was so focused on this dream and I truly believe that he is now living it there in the islands, enjoying the lifestyle he was meant to live. We lost touch with each other but he did take me on a vacation to the area he wanted to live, in the Virgin Islands, and I fell in love with it. He let me share in his dream and it opened up a whole new world for me.

We stayed on the island of Tortola in the British Virgin Islands. The hotel was built around an old sugar cane processing mill that was closed down for years. We stayed in a cabana on stilts right on the beach.

The sounds of the waves lulled me to sleep and the mountainous landscape was lush, green and very peaceful. I was so excited by this adventure that I could hardly contain my enthusiasm.

We rented a Land Rover truck to get around the island and I remember being very frightened of the sharp turns and steep roads that wound their way through this mountainous terrain. One morning we picked up a group of children on their way to school. They were dressed very nicely in their crisp white shirts and navy pants and skirts that made up their school uniforms. I was surprised by their happiness, exuberance and outgoing personalities. They were such a joy to be around and they inspired me, even though they had little wealth, luxury or conveniences. Most of them lived in poverty but they were some of the happiest people I have ever met.

Maybe this was because they lived such an uncomplicated lifestyle in these beautiful surroundings that made them so happy. I could see how this place had become my friend's dream and was happy for him that he had found it and had plans to live it.

I remember watching a movie about a woman in England that goes through a difficult divorce and then decides to leave everything behind and go to Greece.

She gets a job as a waitress in a small seaside restaurant and falls in love with a sexy Greek man. It is such a wonderful change for her and it renews her self-confidence and her spirit.

Sometimes we hold back on living our dream because of fears we have. We are afraid to let go of the familiar and jump out of our safety net. I know this feeling and when I jumped out of my safety net and moved from Chicago to Florida I found out how scary but wonderful it could be.

It was so very surreal when I first came to Florida. It was so different than Chicago. The sunny climate, the Gulf of Mexico, the sandy beaches, instead of cold and snowy winters and overcast skies, were great. The outdoor lifestyle was very different but I loved it. The smaller income was also an adjustment to me. I knew I was worth more in the workplace but Florida jobs didn't pay as well as jobs in Chicago.

It was difficult the first year of living a dream I had always had of moving to Florida. I used to keep seashells on my desk at work when I lived in Chicago, hoping that someday I would be able to realize this dream. I knew that eventually I would live in the tropics after spending many vacations visiting my parents on the Gulf Coast. I thought if I could only figure out a way to work and *retire* before I actually was retirement age, I would move in a heartbeat.

I got my chance when a friend of mine in Chicago was retiring and moving to Naples, Florida. He and I were in a relationship and he was willing to give Florida a chance.

He sold his house in two weeks time and I was not ready to move so quickly but I realized that if I didn't act now, I would never have the courage to do this alone. I gave my two-weeks notice at work and went forward with this adventure.

There were times when I said to myself, what are you doing? Are you crazy? You are giving up any chance at a good career in a big city to go live in a resort, with limited work opportunities. What are you thinking? I agonized over this but still managed to move forward.

I reasoned that if I did not like living in Florida, I could come back to Chicago and start over. I would give it one year and see how I felt at the end of that time.

I was very lucky and landed a job almost as soon as I arrived. I had been sending out resumes and got a call the day after I arrived for an interview. It was with one of the best companies in Naples and I got offered the job the day after my interview.

What a relief! I knew that I was on my way and this was a good sign. At least I would have a way to make a living and also enjoy life by the beach which is one of my favorite places to spend time. I love walking along the beach and now I could do this everyday.

I worked very hard and we found a beautiful home with a pool, surrounded by lush landscaping and a canal in the back of the house.

After the first year, I still was not sure about whether I wanted to continue life in Florida. I told myself that I would give it another year and see what happened. I was working too many hours and getting paid much less than I did in Chicago. My dream was much harder than I thought. I paid a high price for the sunshine, but still thought it was worth it.

As time went on I moved to Fort Myers, found a new home and a more interesting job that paid a higher salary. Then and there I decided that I made the right decision. It was not a perfect place to live, I know now that this does not exist, but it offers many wonderful things I didn't have in Chicago.

I love the winters here and call it our *heaven weather*. During this time you are happy just to walk outside and be alive. It is cooler, sunny, breezy and just beautiful. It renews my spirit and gives me a whole new appreciation for life and the best it has to offer. We never had days like this in Chicago or very few at most.

I do miss many things from the big city though. I miss the culture, diversity, museums, and other events that Chicago had to offer and also the great shopping. I miss the opportunities that I could have had career wise and this is something you have to consider when pursuing a big change like I did.

Don't make a change if you don't have the courage to give some things up that you may never be able to get back and don't put yourself in a situation that you could not recover from if all else fails. Move cautiously but definitely keep your dream alive until you are ready.

All big changes have their pluses and minuses and keep this in mind. You usually have to compromise somewhat in order to make it work out. Even I had to make concessions. Yes, it is getting very crowded, as others have found their way here taking early retirement and looking for a better life. We also have had to deal with hurricanes for the past few years that are scary and yet very interesting. I never thought I would live through some of the weather we have had and the hardships that had followed, with the lack of electricity and supplies, but somehow we all have managed and came out of it better people and survivors.

Speaking of surviving, I had experienced a few of the milder hurricanes, since relocating to Florida, but none of them compared to Hurricane Charley that hit our state in August of 2004.

I rode out the storm in my condominium. It is built very well due to the building requirements becoming much stricter following Hurricane Andrew in 1992. After that storm, residential structures were required to withstand at least 120 mile per hour winds.

I remember bringing in all of my patio furniture inside the night before the storm. I had my portable radio, hurricane lamp, flashlight and batteries all within reach in preparation for the impending bad weather that was predicted to come.

When the storm began, it seemed more interesting than deadly, however, once it progressed, I became more upset and somewhat fearful.

The trees that I could see, when I peeked out of my window, were being blown about by the strong wind and rain. Some were almost facing horizontally from the strength of the wind. I had never experienced this kind of weather and it certainly was an event to remember.

The lake behind my home was usually very calm, but today there were 4-foot waves and whitecaps. The water was being pushed toward my lanai and I thought that it could actually flood my condominium any moment. I thought to myself about what I would do if that happened and figured I would just deal with it by putting towels down and trying to dry everything later. If my whole unit got ruined, then I would just have to accept it and move forward. There was nothing I could do to stop this weather.

I recall talking to my mother, who lives about a half hour away from me in Naples, on my home telephone trying to reassure her while I, myself, was unsure of what was going to happen next. I also had my boyfriend, who also lives in Naples, on the cellular telephone. We all were happy to have each other's support at this time and hoped we could survive to talk about it another day.

As the storm got worse, I went into my interior bathroom, which was supposed to be the safest place to be in the house, according to the local hurricane guidebook. While I was in there I heard the glass on my sliding doors being pushed in and out by the wind. The howling sound will be something I will never forget. I hoped and prayed that the glass would hold out and I wouldn't have to evacuate my home.

At one point, during the storm, the land telephone line went dead and we lost electricity. It got very dark so I turned on my flashlight. I worried about my mother because we lost telephone contact at that point and I hoped she would be all right. She is over eighty years old and lives alone.

I still had contact with my boyfriend on the cell phone but that service went down too. At that moment I felt really alone. I was on my own to weather out the storm with just the survival skills I knew.

The wind was still howling and the rain was blowing in a horizontal direction by the hurricane's force. The storm continued for hours and I wondered how much longer it would be before it would end. I had never seen this kind of power from nature and was both frightened and awed at the same time.

When the storm finally ended, I went outside to survey the damage. It was still very windy but I felt an urgent need to get out of the house.

I saw very large trees totally uprooted. Huge royal palm trees were toppled over, blocking the roadways. There was debris from trees, bushes and metal pieces of framework from homes strewn about. It was devastating to see our paradise so damaged.

As I was walking outside, I started to tremble and thanked God that I was alive. It was as if all of the stress of riding out the storm hit me at once and my body shook with relief that it was finally over. I was happy that the storm had not been worse and that my home was intact.

My Florida dream did not include this type of experience but it taught me so much about living and survival that I feel fortunate to have gone through it.

We were without electricity for four days. I had no air conditioning in the 90-degree heat, no hot water and had lost all of the food in my refrigerator but I was still here and my mother and boyfriend were fine too. This was the most important thing as everything else could be dealt with over time.

I took cold showers by candlelight and made do with canned tuna and peanut butter and jelly sandwiches for a few days. It was just another new adventure to me.

Keep this in mind when you face obstacles on your way to living your dream. Realize that you may be faced with hardships and challenges along the way. Learn to become resourceful and to accept help from others when needed.

Do not give up so easily when problems arise. The challenges make us grow as people and give us self-confidence as we go about solving the problems that can arise. We also learn that other people can be a wonderful resource for you.

Following Hurricane Charley, the people in this area really came together to provide assistance to each other. Neighbors helped others clean up their lawns, repair each other's houses and provided food and water to people who needed it.

In the subdivision where I live, the neighbors fired up the outdoor barbeque grill, near our swimming pool clubhouse, and everyone brought over food. The food needed to be cooked right away because it had thawed out from the power outages taking out the refrigeration. The residents had a big cookout and shared camaraderie, support and storm horror stories with each other.

I am glad I lived my Florida dream and I hope to live out more dreams as the future unfolds for me. I want you to live your dreams too. Anything that is worthwhile takes a firm commitment, a good plan and lots of fortitude to see it through. The outcome is worth your efforts and realizing your dream can be one of the most fulfilling events in your life.

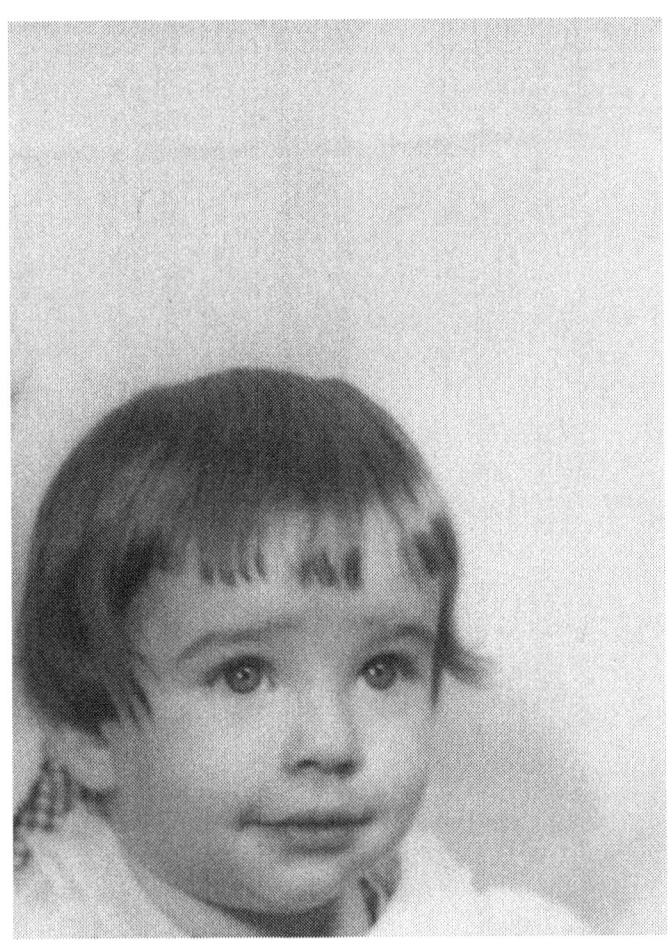

Myself as a chubby baby.

This is the garden in our back yard when I was growing up. It was my favorite grazing spot for organic food.

I loved animals even at a very young age. This was our dog Fritz and my neighbor friend Helen's cat.

This was graduation day from Elmhurst College and one of my proudest
moments.

High School Graduation

My older sister Betty and brother Tom in front of the trailer that was my first home

Me having fun at Disney World and being a kid again

Lighthouse Beach in Sanibel, Florida that is one of my favorite beach walking areas

More Sanibel beach

Imagine yourself here

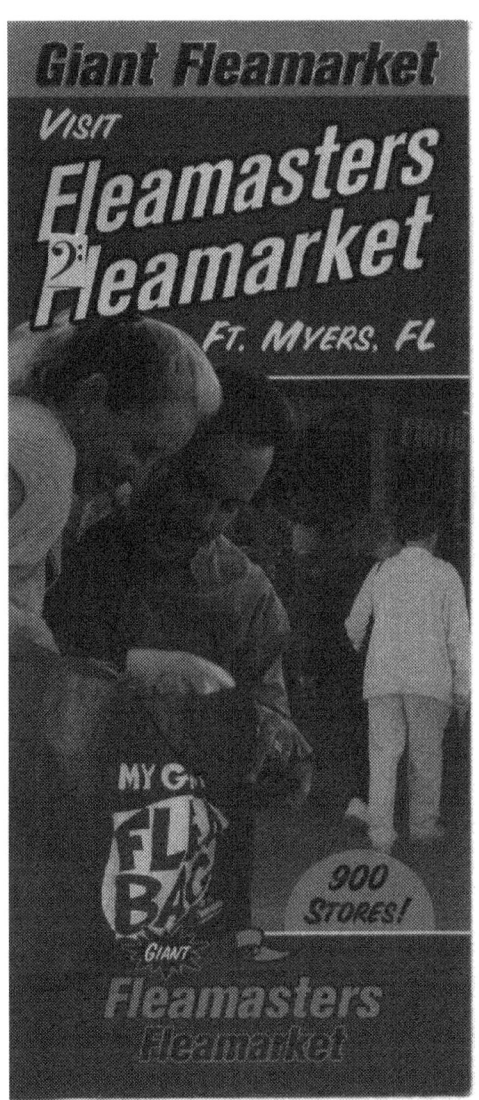

The Flea Market with many great adventures

Flea Market Birds

Flea Market Vegetables

Tasty Flea Market Food

Flea Market Flowers

Myself at age 50

Myself in My 40's

Myself in My 30's

Myself in My 20's

My Parrot Nicki

Future Avocado Tree

My Tortola Adventure

My Grandmother who I thought was very beautiful

7

FINANCES

As a child I was taught by my parents to save money. Both of them, like many parents of the baby boomers of my generation, had lived through the Depression era and had a strong sense of the value of a dollar. At a very young age, they took me to the bank for my first passbook savings account. What a thrill it was to get that little book and to get paid for putting money into the bank. What a novel idea earning interest was to me as a child. Getting more money from my original money was very motivating. It inspired me to save even more money that I made from babysitting and other jobs.

I have always been conscious of saving money but it was very difficult as a young, single mother trying to raise my son on my own. It wasn't until I was in my mid-forties that I realized that in order to retire someday, I had to concentrate on building a nest egg.

I am not a PHD in finance. My background is in business and I did work as an accountant for a number of years. I learned early on how money can earn you more money and how a conservative spending mode can bring its own rewards.

I got all the books I could on finance and investing and even though it was difficult, I forced myself to learn all I could about the stock market, securities, bonds compound interest and money markets.

Early in my career I had the opportunity to work for individuals with money to invest and I learned that it took money to make money. If you can just get that first deposit, you can add to it and make it grow. My mother has a term for it. She says her money is *making babies*.

I really like this concept and it can inspire you to save so your money can make babies too!

It is not easy to get that first dollar amount. You must sacrifice immediate pleasure for future security and growth. Once you get enough invested you can allow more immediate gratification, but until you have enough, you must be focused on your goal.

What is enough? My first goal was $100,000. It was a real stretch for me to imagine meeting this goal. My annual income was in the $20,000–$30,000 range. I had some money saved, approximately $26,000 when I was in my mid-forties in 1993. By 1996 I had $86,000 and in 2001 I had over $200,000 in investments. Today this has more than doubled and it amazes me the power of investing even just a few dollars and where it can take you.

How did I do this? One thing is I was very motivated. I had moved to Florida in 1993 and I encountered many retired people. I wondered how they were able to retire and not have to work. I was envious as I went to work each day while they were going to play tennis, golf or go to the beach. I envisioned myself in their place in the future and this vision gave me the incentive to reach for my financial goals.

I have to say that I was fortunate to be investing during a period when the market was strong and growing. Timing can be very critical when investing, but I was thinking long term and knew that the stock market was vulnerable and that it really was a long-term investment. I knew that to be successful, I would have to diversify and utilize both safe and somewhat risky sources of investing.

I am not a big risk taker. I work too hard for my money to just see it blow away. Because of this, my portfolio will grow slower, but I know what my risk limit is and you have to find a comfort zone in which you can live.

One good investment I did make was buying my condominium. I had previously worked in the real estate business in the suburbs of Chicago and initially in residential apartment management. Later on I graduated into commercial real estate and remodeling and construction work.

Because of this background, over twenty years in the business, I was one of the pickiest customers when it came to finding a home to buy. I wanted to see how the buildings were constructed and I studied the best locations and areas where I thought the properties would appreciate the most.

It took me three years to finally find a place that I felt would serve me well both as a home and as a sound financial investment.

One of the reasons it took me so long to purchase was that I was so disappointed in most of the construction work. I expect a good product and I was not seeing it. I saw roofs that were being put up with plywood that was too thin to support the cement roof tiles that were being placed on top of it. This roof would not stand up to the test of time and would start leaking in a few years causing the owner additional expenses and headaches because they were not aware of this defect in construction.

Also, many of the homes had an inside plumbing system bringing water to areas of the house in what looked like gray garden hose. I had never seen this before because I was used to regular metal piping or PVC pipe. I wondered how sturdy this gray hose was and thought about what a nightmare it would be if it began to leak behind the walls. This could happen after a few years due to the cheap nature of this product. The builders figured that the customer would not be aware of what was actually behind the walls and wouldn't suspect that they were receiving an inferior water system. I was appalled at what the builders were getting away with and was disappointed at the quality I was seeing out in the new developments.

It seemed like the more I looked at, the more disappointed I became. I even gave up my search a few times and decided to just rent since I did not feel that the housing I was looking at was worth investing in at all.

I even saw houses that, instead of using plywood as facing under the face brick or stucco, they were using Styrofoam sheets. I noticed that homes that had this kind of installation would look terrible on the outside after only two or three years. Water would get behind the Styrofoam and it would turn black, crack and break up making the house look very unattractive and creating a big expense for the person buying it. In most cases, the entire face of the house would have to be replaced.

Other homes were built in areas that were too close to major power line towers, garbage dumps and in swampy areas prone to flooding. I believe that homes should not be constructed in areas like this because many buyers are not aware of these hazards and suffer disappointment and financial losses by learning of these disadvantages after they purchase and move in.

A home is a very important part of a person's life and you should really educate yourself or take someone with you that can help you when you decide to purchase this kind of an investment.

Many people today are carrying too much debt. It is so easy to buy anything with charge cards without feeling the direct impact of the spending like you do with cash, a debit card or with a check. This large debt not only affects a person's household, but also the economy as a whole. It is like the massive debt owed by the Federal Government. It keeps growing with no end in sight.

Individuals need to try to get a handle on their debt, but this is not easy and not without some will power and changing of your idea of what you *need* rather than just what you *want*.

When I purchased my home, I wanted to go out and buy new furniture and make it a showplace that would be impressive to my friends and beautiful to me. I knew I didn't have the money to do this and did not want to go into unnecessary debt so I decided to just fix up what I could and buy some nice accessories to dress up what I already had. This worked out fine and whenever I get a little extra money, I just buy one good piece of furniture or other accent pieces to upgrade my home. This takes great will power and is very difficult. There are times when I just feel like I want to replace everything but then I get my investment statements and see that I have made thousands of dollars in interest and I quickly change my mind.

Don't worry about impressing your friends too much with what you have. Good friends will love you for yourself and not what you have. If your friends are disappointed in you because you don't have the best of everything, lose them. Your companionship and love should be enough and if it is not, they are not worth having as friends.

Many people today don't blink an eye about having a $30,000 balance on multiple charge cards. They buy bigger houses to store what they have charged and have to work harder to pay for all of their purchases. This affects their quality of life and they have little time to enjoy what they have and their families because they are working so hard. A vicious cycle is created by the buy, spend and work to pay it all off result that can be difficult to end.

Don't get lured into the debt prison. We all want nice things, new cars, big beautiful homes, designer clothes and the best of everything but you must be careful and live within your means.

When I went to purchase my condominium the realtors kept steering me to more expensive houses. I told them what my price limit was but they kept telling me that I qualified for twice the mortgage that I was seeking. Most people would give in to this and buy the more expensive home but I stuck to my comfortable price range.

Believe me it was difficult. The more expensive houses looked wonderful, but I had everything calculated down to the penny so I knew what I felt comfortable with as far as the debt was concerned.

This is an important step in purchasing anything. Know what your budget is ahead of time. Having an accounting and business background has helped me with compiling budgets. If you cannot do this yourself, get some assistance before you go out to purchase. It is a good idea because there are other factors you may never even consider when purchasing large items such as a home.

An example of a simple budget is the following. Make two columns on a piece of paper as follows:

SAMPLE BUDGET

INCOME		EXPENSES	
Salary, Wages	$_____	Housing	$_____
Interest Income	$_____	Automobile	$_____
Other Income	$_____	Utilities	$_____
		Food	$_____
		Cable TV & Internet Service	$_____
		Clothing	$_____
		Recreation	$_____
		Insurance(homeowners, auto, life)	$_____
		Savings	$_____
		Miscellaneous	$_____
Total Income	**$**	**Total Expenses**	**$**

This is a very simplified budget but is still very effective at managing your money. Just fill in the dollar amounts to the best of your knowledge and add more income or expense categories if you find that you need them. You will be very surprised at what you will see. Most people have more expenses than income. How do they do it then? Well, in fact, most live off of their credit cards and do not even realize it until they do this exercise. Others just keep putting off payments each month hoping for a windfall.

Many people do not want to know where their money is going and never consider ahead of time how a large purchase will affect their financial status.

Before making any large purchase, you should check your budget and see if it will work. If it creates too much debt, don't do it. It is better to save for that item and put off the instant gratification it gives than to deal with all of the pressure that heavy debt brings with it.

If you can't pay it off at the end of the month, do not purchase the item with a charge card. This requires good discipline, but believe me it will save you from getting in over your head. Save the money and purchase the item when you can pay for it in full.

There are exceptions to this rule and you need to be flexible at times. Large purchases such as automobiles, television sets, furniture and emergency repairs cannot always be paid for immediately and may need to be paid on a payment plan. Just try to pay these expenses off as soon as possible and negotiate a good interest rate for the loan. Take good care of these items after purchasing them so that they will last a long time and you don't have to replace them as often.

When planning for retirement, find a good financial planner you can trust. Look for one that works independently. This means that he is not affiliated with just one investment company, but can steer you to a wider variety of investments and can give you better advice on what type of investments will work for you.

You may have to pay for this service, but it is money well spent. If you cannot find a financial planner or investment counselor, many tax accountants can also provide this service.

Remember to make your money work for you in order to make it grow. Spend wisely and keep your debt under control. You will have a higher standard of living as you age and less worry about having enough funding for the future and to last a lifetime.

8

BEAUTY

In our youth-obsessed society, it is difficult to imagine beauty at fifty years old and beyond but beauty can be found and even as we change. We can enhance our beauty with a little help from natural makeup and a less is more philosophy.

As we age, our skin becomes thinner and the layer of collagen under it lessens and we see some wrinkling and sagging. There are ways to camouflage these areas to make them less noticeable.

First of all, a good moisturizer is very important. This will protect the skin and soften wrinkles so they are less noticeable. I use Elizabeth Arden Visible Difference refining moisture cream and have used it for many years. It is a miracle in a jar. I also love Key West Aloe's Night Moist cream for nighttime use. During the daytime I use an Aloe Moisturizing Crème with Vitamins E, A & D by Earthly Elements. You can find this cream in health food stores. I also love the Estee Lauder face creams. I haven't found one I don't like and they make my skin look wonderful. I have provided a list at the end of this book with sources to purchase the items that I recommend.

Finding a lighter weight foundation also helps. Heavy foundation accumulates in wrinkles and crevices and makes them appear more evident. Revlon Age Defying liquid makeup is a great one. I also love Estee Lauder Equalizer liquid makeup. It is made for combination skin, but I love the way it doesn't accumulate in lines and wrinkles which is a plus for us who have passed the age of fifty. Another great makeup is Estee Lauder's Ideal Matte Makeup which gives great coverage and makes your skin look flawless.

These are just a few makeup choices. Experiment until you find one that works for you. Don't be afraid to ask for a make over at a department store cosmetic counter or from a beauty consultant. Also, many beauty salons have makeup artists that will do your makeup for you. If you like what you see, ask them where you can get the products and for instructions on how to use them.

Cream blushes, I feel, are better to use as we age. It is easier to blend and places less of a pulling and tugging on your already delicate skin. This kind of blush also gives you a rosey, healthy glow that gives a more youthful appearance. I use Revlon's Age Defying Cheek Color. It is just wonderful.

When I want a more dramatic and fashion model finished look, I use Adrian Arpel's Signature Club A line of products. I found them on the Home Shopping Network television program and they are worth their weight in gold. All of her products make you look much younger and are really geared toward the woman over forty. They make you look like a model every time.

The eyes are another area where we can create a more youthful look. Putting a light beige color on the brow bone can brighten deeper set eyes that may have some loose eyelid skin. Soft pastel colors work better as we get older. Leave the dark colors to the younger girls. Lavender, mauve and light brown colors work best. Again I recommend Adrian Arpel's signature line. She has the perfect colors in powders, creams and liquids.

I also love Aziza eye shadows. They are inexpensive, blend well and come in packages with three colors already coordinated to look well together. They give great instructions on where to put each color on your eyelid in order to make the application go easier.

Thinning eyelashes can be a problem when we age. They can however be enhanced with the special mascara that builds body. I use Loreal's 1,000 Calorie Mascara. It doesn't smudge all day and washes off easily with soap and water. Also, find a good eyelash curler. Some work better than others at curling your lashes. Curling the lashes really opens up your eyes and this is important because as we age our eyelids have a tendency to get heavier and the years of gravitational pull make them sag.

In order to combat that "sleepy eye" look, working with shadows and mascara is essential. Light beiges on the brow bone really bring that area forward. Curling the lashes and using mascara puts the focus on the lashes rather than the lids.

I like to use eyeliner in a variety of colors. My favorite is a lighter blue that adds softness to the face and gives a more youthful appearance. I also use a dark olive green, deep purple and gray. This gives me a nice variety of looks that keeps the eyes more interesting and vibrant.

Using blue instead of black mascara is a good trick too. It gives you a whole new look and draws attention to the eyes, especially if they are blue or green like mine.

Another helpful hint for using makeup to correct the signs of aging is using a darker foundation on the hollows of the cheeks that will create a thinner facial appearance and using it at the jaw line and under, where we sometimes develop jowls. This is a great way to camouflage signs of aging and give you a more youthful appearance.

Outlining of the lips is a wonderful way to keep lipstick from bleeding and escaping into the vertical cracks around our mouth that form as we age. Pick a color for the liner that is close to your lipstick color so you don't see an actual line drawn around your lips. When you see the line it is distracting and doesn't look natural. Select colors that are not too dark or light. Use medium tones in neutral, mauve, rose and caramel colors.

I use more than one color of lipstick because I can never find just one color that is right for me. For the base, I use a matte color, usually closest to my natural color, but a little darker. Then, on top of that, I use a sheerer, iridescent color to soften the appearance. This shiny top color gives a look of a more contemporary woman and camouflages small lip lines.

The natural lip color that we were born with fades over time and it is important to reapply lip color often so you don't have that washed out look. You would be surprised at what a difference a little lip touch up makes in your overall youthful appearance.

Eyebrows are an important area that we don't want to neglect. They can really brighten up your whole face. My sister sent me a wonderful product from Smashbox Cosmetics for the eyebrows that may work for you. My eyebrows have thinned out over time and I need to fill them in and give them more definition. This product is a powder shadow and wax sealer that is applied with an angled brush. It looks very natural when applied and brings a nicely finished look to the face. It is easy to control how much is applied and if you make a mistake, you can easily wipe it off.

One problem area I have that is very aging is my neck. I am getting what is referred to as *turkey neck*. Nothing against turkeys, it looks fine on them but on humans it can be a nightmare and really make you look older. The skin on my neck has become looser and hangs down a bit. This really bothers me and, I feel, ages me greatly. I lift weights to tone the neck area which helps with the sagging. I use turtleneck sweaters and shirts and scarves tied around my neck to cover it. I think that I look much more youthful when I can cover my neck. I love the kind of collars the women wore in the 1800's when they wore decorative, lacy ones all the way up to their chins!

Our ideas of beauty are so restrictive. We seem to only recognize perfection and what is handed down to us in the media as the ideal that we should all strive to achieve. However, I would like to celebrate all kinds of beauty. I find beauty where there is not perfection and truly believe that beauty is ageless.

When I was a little girl I used to go with my parents to Wisconsin to visit my maternal grandmother and namesake Mary. I loved going to visit her because she was such a profound presence. She didn't realize it but I got an impression of strength and independence that stayed with me and helped me form my own attitudes and resiliency.

Grandmother was in her eighties, tall, white-haired and wore very loose fitting dresses without belts. She hated belts because they were so confining and to this day, I hate belts too.

Grandmother was not beautiful in the high fashion model sense of today's culture but to me, a five year old at the time, she was the most beautiful person I knew. At five or six years old you have not been influenced by society's and media's emphasis on stick-thin, made up, surgery enhanced ideals of beauty. You are innocent to this and are free to see real beauty both inward and outward.

My grandmother's hair was long and white and she wore it twisted under in a bun at the back of her head. Her face was lined and she had very large ears with extremely long lobes. Her face told her story, many years of working outside on the farm, raising fourteen children and losing a husband in her forties when a bull on the farm attacked and killed him. Hers was not an easy life.

I found her face mesmerizing and was fascinated and drawn to it. It impressed me and it never occurred to me that she was not a beauty. I had no preconceived ideas of what beauty was, no influences from the media, so she, to me was a great beauty and still is today as a memory in my heart.

Grandmother was a feisty, down-to-earth woman who had false teeth that she used to keep in an olive jar on her wood-burning stove. When we would first arrive at her house for visits she would say, "wait a minute, I have to put my choppers in," referring to her teeth. I thought this was really cool that she could take her teeth in and out whenever she wanted. I couldn't do that so I was very impressed. Oh the naivety of children! It really makes you realize how when we are older, things like this are repulsive, but to an innocent child, can be fascinating.

We would go fishing up in the lakes of Wisconsin while we were visiting grandmother and bring her back all of these fish to cook. She would jump right in and clean the fish like a pro. She would bring out this large cast iron pan and put some lard into it and cook the fish. It tasted so wonderful!

Grandmother never worried about her wrinkles, weight, money, looks or success. She was a survivor who accepted life as it came and used her basic skills to survive and take care of herself. She lived well into her nineties without concern about cholesterol, weight gain, plastic surgery, cancer, heart disease, putting on makeup, wearing designer clothes or the fact that she was by herself for much of her life. She accepted the seasons of life just like we accept the seasons of nature and set a good example for the rest of us.

She and her life have always been an inspiration and guideline for me in my own life. I find myself, on many occasions, asking how would grandmother have handled this situation and act in a way I think she would have approved. She had many experiences and handled the tough times that life had dealt her with instinctive survival skills, grace and her own dynamic and perseverant spirit.

Don't worry too much about your wrinkles and other signs of aging. Remember that each year of your life is a gift to be enjoyed. You earned those wrinkles and it is your right to show them off! Our society and the media put so much emphasis on the young and their beauty. We don't see enough advertising and focus on the middle-aged women and beyond. This is unfortunate because it sends a negative message about aging. It makes people feel sad about losing their youthful appearance when instead they should be emphasizing the wonderful aspects of getting older. Granted, we all want to be beautiful forever, but this is not possible and we cannot afford to waste any time or energy lamenting the past and trying aimlessly to look like we are twenty-five forever.

I have a very good friend whose mother is in her nineties, yet she is one of the most beautiful and gracious women I know. She always has her hair done very nicely, wears elegant clothing, has a thin figure and the warmest handshake and smile I have ever seen. I admire her immensely and I tell her so. She deserves this and deserves to know that someone does appreciate all of her beauty whether youthful or not.

This woman attended law school in the days when ninety-nine percent of the students attending were men. She married a man who was a widower with four children and raised them as if they were her own.

She continues to practice law to this day and in spite of her ninety plus years and failing eyesight! She attends the opera whenever she can and loves outdoor concerts.

She is a true inspiration to me and all who know her and her beauty is truly ageless.

Keep this image in mind when you look into the mirror instead of the one the youth-obsessed media tries to push on us.

When I was younger I always thought that I needed to be the most beautiful woman in the room. I would feel such great pressure to pick the best outfit, have my hair perfectly coifed and my makeup flawlessly applied.

I would change outfits over and over again hoping to find the one that would be noticed and have the greatest impact on those that saw me. I worked on my hair to try to make sure to impress. I love makeup and would put on eye shadow, liner, foundation, blush, lipstick and mascara. It had to be glamorous, gorgeous and attractive enough to turn heads.

I would feel inadequate otherwise. Even after all of the work of preparation, I would still wonder whether I was good enough. Low self-esteem would creep up and even if I was satisfied with my look, I had my doubts.

As I grew older, this pressure disappeared. I had the confidence and self-esteem earned from living life and surviving. I no longer had to be the most attractive woman in the room. I was finally comfortable with who I was and what I had become as a woman.

I still pay close attention to dressing and making my hair and makeup the best it can be, but it isn't the end of the world if I am not the prettiest girl in the room. I am content with just being me.

Can you imagine the pressure I put on myself just trying so hard to be perfect, to be wanted and be approved by all who saw me! I am very happy to have left that pressure behind me and concentrate on more important things.

This is a great accomplishment and I am so relieved that this happened. I can now walk into a room, head held high even if my hair, makeup and clothes are not perfect. I, myself, am good enough. My personality, knowledge and kindness make a much better impact than physical beauty.

Instead of focusing on myself, I decided to make a point of making others feel good about themselves. I easily gave compliments and it all away to others. I would find something about those I met to compliment them on and make them feel wonderful.

I did not want others to feel what I did for so long, not knowing if I was attractive or good enough. No one told me so I thought there must be something wrong with me. I had terrible self-doubts and wondered what I could do to feel wanted.

I used men's feedback as a barometer of my attractiveness. I thought that if I got attention and their interest in a room or walking down the street, then I must be beautiful and attractive. If I didn't get attention, then I must be ugly, dreadful and worthless! I could go from pure euphoria to the depths of despair solely on the feedback I received from men.

As I got older I realized what a mistake this was, going through these highs and lows and stopped relying on other's impressions of me. I learned that I was the one who needed to find the beauty, attractiveness and worthiness in myself. This meant seeing more than just the physical aspects of beauty, but knowing that beauty encompasses so much more of your total being.

The beauty we bring to the world should be in presenting the best person we can be. Taking care of our health, dressing in the best way we can afford, making an effort to have powerful energy, generous spirit and joy in living should be our priorities.

You will have this if you use your life to not only take care of yourself, but to give to others through community service, volunteering and just sharing all the wonderful knowledge you have gained over years of experience. What you have learned in the course of your life can be shared with others. This is a gift you can pass on to future generations.

No, I no longer scan the room to see who is noticing me. Are the men taking an interest? Will they like me? It doesn't matter like it used to in my youth. I know who I am. I know I have some attractiveness, even now in my fifties. It isn't the great, knockout beauty of youth, but that has diminished in importance to me. I don't need that anymore.

Oh, I still love that smiling glance of approval from men, but it does not define me as it once did. I appreciate it, thank God for it and get a big kick out of it more than anything else. I know that even if I don't get noticed my self-esteem will remain intact and I am still a worthwhile person.

The day is going to come when you are no longer the hot young chick or young stud. Youth only comes once in a lifetime. Enjoy it while you have it and don't take it for granted. Don't walk around being arrogant and frowning on older folks as I see young people do from time to time. Remember that one day you will walk in their shoes and keep this in mind.

Instead look on the older population with respect and awe that they made it to middle age and beyond. This is quite a feat in itself. Age has it's own beauty and wisdom and should be admired.

Baby boomers should celebrate every wrinkle and every sag, knowing they are survivors and very unique people who have lived, loved and enjoyed every year.

Yes, you can admire the young people with their youth knowing that you too experienced that time of life. Remember it and love the time you are in. Your experience and wisdom gained by living is worth much more than the youth of yesterday. Believe this and your true beauty will shine through always.

9

HOBBIES

I have always had hobbies and they really can showcase your talents and raise your self-esteem, bring fun and a great sense of accomplishment too.

My favorite hobby of all time is definitely shopping. Ever since I was a teenager, I loved to go to our local shopping center. Like the lioness that I am, I have always enjoyed the hunt for great clothes and bargains. After all, we come from ancestors that were hunter-gatherers and we were meant to go out in search of our needs. Since we don't need to hunt for our food, we need to obtain other items in order to fulfill this need. It is in our genetic makeup and we are compelled to do it. This may be why we get such a wonderful sense of satisfaction when we find that fantastic bargain and arrive home, admiring all of our fabulous finds. We take them out and admire our choices and savor the successful hunt just like the lioness.

I can tell when I need an excursion to the mall. I get restless, irritable, hyperactive and need my shopping fix. The worst of times is when a holiday comes around and all of the stores are closed. Those are difficult times and thank goodness for Walgreens and Seven-Elevens that are open for business on those days. I can spend an hour in a Walgreens store. First I check out all of the new makeup. I can always find items I can't locate anywhere else. Then I peruse all of the fashion magazines and last but not least, I check out the candy aisle and food section. Thank you Walgreens for being there when I need you most!

The only other person I know who loves shopping, even more than me, is my sister. I remember one Christmas season when she came to visit me in Florida from her home state of California. We shopped all day. At one point I had gotten so tired that I sat right down on the floor in one of the stores because I couldn't stand up any longer. However, my sister was not tired at all. She was still going strong and hadn't missed a beat. Now that is power shopping!

It got to be around nine in the evening and the stores were closing. My sister was so disappointed that we would have to end our shopping spree. I had to think quickly, and as tired as I was, I remembered that we had a local Wal-Mart store that was open 24 hours a day. I mentioned this to my sister and she was thrilled. We headed over there and spent at least another two hours finding more treasures.

This sounds excessive, but we really had a great time and felt totally satisfied, albeit exhausted, afterwards.

I also love to sew. I have very little free time to do this, but from time to time I find things I see that inspire me to sew.

A number of years ago I actually made my husband, (later ex-husband), an entire suit. I remember it well because it was such an ambitious project to take on at the time. It was a brown, denim-like material and I used toggle buttons, instead of traditional buttons to make it look very unique and stylish. My husband wore it for a number of years and then I handed it down to my younger brother who also looked very handsome in it.

I also sewed all of my maternity clothes when I was pregnant with my son. We didn't have much money and I did not want to waste money on a wardrobe I only was going to wear once. It was fun making the maternity clothes too. I remember getting so excited during the process and couldn't wait to wear my new creations.

Find a sewing center in your area and see if they give lessons or just get a good sewing book like I did.

Hobbies like these aren't just enjoyable. They actually enhance your self-esteem. You feel good about the fact that you created something you can wear and you did it all yourself, having fun in the process.

Another favorite hobby is growing things, especially plants and flowers. Living in Florida makes this very easy because we have an abundance of sunshine and rain, but you can do this hobby in most any climate.

My mother, who is a great inspiration to me, has many avocado trees on her property and most of them were started from seeds. She got me hooked on avocado plants because they are very interesting to grow and grow very quickly.

After you eat the wonderfully delicious fruit of the avocado, take the entire seed and remove any loose brown skin from it. Take four (4) tooth-picks and put them into the seed by twisting them into the seed about halfway down around it so the four toothpicks are at the same level. You have to be very careful how you put the toothpicks in so they don't break. Twisting them carefully helps the process.

Then place the seed, flat side down, into a cup or glass of water, making sure that at least half of the seed is submerged into the water. Change the water daily and in a few weeks you will see roots growing out of the bottom of the seed.

When the roots get to be about two (2) inches long, transfer the seed into a good size clay pot and least nine (9) inches across and twelve (12) inches deep.

Place large stones or clay shards at the bottom of the pot, making sure you cover the hole at the bottom. This will allow for good drainage when watering. Place enough potting soil in the pot and leave a few inches at the top for the seed. Make an indentation in the soil and place the seed, root side down, into the potting soil gently without damaging the roots.

Fill in more potting soil around the seed and leave about an inch of seed at the top exposed. Water this plant well and place it where it can get some sunshine.

After a few weeks, you will see the seed start to split open at the top and tiny green shoots will emerge. Every day the shoots will grow taller and later become branches with bright green leaves. This plant grows very fast and that is what makes it so much fun to grow.

I have started so many of these plants that are so beautiful and lush and I give them to friends and co-workers to plant in their yards. They make great house warming gifts.

When my son was 19 years old he left home for the first time and enlisted into the United States Coast Guard. It was a difficult time for me because I really missed him. It had just been the two of us for so many years, since I divorced his dad when he was about 4 years old and I not only lost my son but what was my family. He and I were together for all of those years and it was hard to see him go off into the world.

A friend of mine decided that I needed a "new baby." He bought me an African Grey parrot hatchling and gave it to me as a gift. He knew I loved birds and thought that I would have fun raising it. This was the beginning of a new hobby for me.

I had to hand feed my new baby bird three times a day, carefully mixing the formula and feeding it with a small syringe. This was very challenging because the bird did not want to always sit still and sometimes would even fall asleep as I was feeding it but it was fun and I really loved this new adventure.

It was scary at times because I was afraid of making the formula too hot, feeding her too much or dropping her. It was a big responsibility but I felt up to the challenge.

This wasn't a substitute for my son but it took my mind off of his absence when I was caring for my new hatchling.

I named her Nicki and it was so much fun raising her. She was so cute and playful and it was so much fun watching her grow into such a beautiful and talkative bird.

This hobby expanded as I added some other new birds to my menagerie. I had a Moluccan Cockatoo parrot, an Orange Winged Amazon parrot and another African Grey parrot named "Maggie." I also raised a baby wild sparrow that was found by the beach and had fallen from its nest.

I learned many things raising my birds. I had to be very patient and it was very similar to raising children. They require lots of food, lots of cleanup, tender loving care and much love and attention.

I read a number of books and joined some bird clubs where I met other bird lovers and made some interesting friends. At the bird shows I got to see so very many different types of birds and it opened up a whole new world to me.

My birds brought me great joy and fun and helped me through the "empty nest" period when my son left home. I got a whole new nest full of new babies to take care of and it turned out to be a great hobby for me.

Having hobbies gives us pleasure and an outlet in which to show our creativity. It always amazes me just how creative people are and what they can produce. Take a moment to find a good hobby for yourself and see what you too can create.

10

STRESS REDUCTION

Stress reduction, I believe, is very important to maintaining our health. Studies have been done that affirm this and your entire well-being is affected by stress.

We live in a stressful world and there is no way to totally avoid stress, but we must do what we can to control it and manage it because it has a profound effect on our health. Recent studies have shown this and I believe it plays a role in early death.

I have experienced many stressful events and can personally back up this claim. When I got divorced, I lost over twenty pounds because I was worried about having enough money, raising my son alone and whether I could survive and thrive on my own without the support and help from a spouse. Everywhere I looked I saw couples and I felt like I was the only single person left on the face of the earth. I had to learn all over again how to regain my self-esteem and know that I still was a wonderful, beautiful, accomplished person who could find love again, find success and become a whole person capable of great things.

At the time, I dealt with the stress by crying and busying myself to the point of exhaustion. This was not good, but I had not yet learned about the benefits of proper diet and exercise and how that would have helped.

My diet at this time contained too much sugar that fueled my anxiety and restlessness. I learned through trial and error, and by educating myself about good nutrition later in life, how diet plays such an important role in feeling anxious and depressed. We have a tendency to reach for comfort foods during periods of anxiety and stress and this is not a good idea.

I learned through research that I needed to eat complex carbohydrates, stay away from caffeine and sugar and not let myself get too hungry in order to stabilize my moods. This helped me tremendously and can greatly assist you during stressful periods.

I noticed a big difference in my sleep patterns after I limited just the caffeine and sugar. I stopped all caffeinated beverages except for one cup of coffee in the morning and have kept this practice to this day.

It helped me actually sleep through a whole night, which I had not been able to do for a long time. Before I would wake up at 2:00 AM in the morning, wide-awake and not able to go back to sleep. I would be processing all of the responsibilities I had and overwhelmed myself with feelings of terror. At that point I would just get up and start doing things just to get my mind on something else.

Actually this was a good thing and I recommend it to anyone who is going through a stressful period. Getting your body moving and taking action can improve your mood and give you back your sense of control.

At least that is what I felt when I would get up and get busy. The only problem I would have later was that I had gotten up so early but by the early evening hours I was ready for bed but had too many things left to do to be able to just turn in for the evening.

Another trick I would use when I would lie awake at 2:00 AM was to get up and read something. It would take my mind off of my own worries and anxieties and focus it on what I was reading. People Magazine was one of my favorites. I loved reading about other people, their lives, accomplishments, successes and failures. I learned many things from the experiences of others.

Remember also to take time off from work. When I do this, I begin to feel like a human being again, instead of just a machine that just keeps going and going, afraid to rest or I may never get up again.

I use time off to catch up on things I need to do around the house, clean out closets, wash windows, run errands and do all those things you never seem to have enough time to do when your are working. This takes the pressure off of you by knowing that you don't have all these projects looming over you that need to be done. You can rejoice in finishing them and unleash yourself from this burden.

I usually mix in some mini getaways to some of my favorite local spots. I live in one of the most beautiful places in the world and don't have to go to far from home to find great vacation areas.

I get up early in the morning and drive down to Naples, Florida which is about a half-hour trip, and go walk the beach near the Naples Pier.

I love to take long walks on the beach and also check out what is going on at the pier. There are always fishermen catching fish and I always run into someone I know to talk to and pass the time with while enjoying the blue water, warm sunshine and cool breezes. This relaxes me and renews my spirit in a way that no drug or other substance can do. I bask in the warm sunlight and thank God for all he has given me including these wonderful moments.

Sanibel Island and Captiva, Florida are other places that I go to relax and enjoy life. Just driving over the bridge to get to Sanibel Island is such a beautiful treat. You see all of the different shades of blue and green that make up the water in the Gulf of Mexico and the white sand looks like mounds of sugar that go on for miles. I marvel at all of the beautiful homes that line the shore and wonder about all of the people that live in them. What a treat it would be to be able to live right on the beach. Seeing all of this is such a wonderful experience and it immediately makes me calm all over just to be in this special place.

There are two beaches that I go to walk on the island and both are very different. The one by the lighthouse is nice to walk because I can go into the water and walk pretty far out without it getting very deep or rough. I take my shoes off and let the sand seep between my toes and feel the soft, cool water that is so very refreshing. Just walking and meditating brings me relief from the stresses of day-to-day living and transports me to a warm and calming place.

Further up the island is Captiva and driving there is a treat in itself. The winding roads and views of the water and landscaping are breathtaking. There are colorful buildings and areas with very interesting structures that are like nowhere else. It is a unique and welcoming setting that I always feel privileged to be able to visit and experience.

This is my therapy for stress and it really works for me. You can find places right near where you live to go to have these kinds of getaways and relieve your stress. Seek out these places and frequent them as much as you can in order to find relief and bring a sense of calmness in your life.

How you view the world and the people in it can affect your levels of stress and relief from it. When you are feeling low and all seems to be going wrong and the stress builds to a point where you start to panic and feel that all is lost, remember that no matter what happens, you are loved.

Take a moment to think about those people that have loved you and helped you unconditionally.

I remember one Christmas season when my son was five or six years old. I had been divorced not quite one year and we were just getting by financially. We lived in an apartment with little or no heat and experienced more than one sewer backup in our unit.

The holiday season was approaching and I did not have enough money for a Christmas tree but I managed to buy a few gifts for my son.

There was a man I had just met who was a pharmacist. My son liked him and called him the six million dollar man, because that was a hit show at the time. My son looked at my friend as a hero because he was so good to us.

He would never come and visit empty handed. He made a good salary and knew we had little so he took great pride in helping us. He was just what we both needed at the time. Not just because he brought us things but because he thought enough of us to do this for us. This made us feel good about ourselves, that this wonderful man thought so highly of us and wanted to share his life and assistance.

A few days before Christmas he showed up with a Christmas tree, lights, ornaments, a train set and other toys for my son that he purchased from the store that he worked at as a pharmacist.

I remember the look of joy on his face when I opened my door and saw him with all his gifts. He loved being able to treat us and I couldn't believe that there was someone that really cared about us and our happiness that Christmas.

He came into my apartment with all of the boxes and started putting the tree together. We decorated it and then, even though he was tired from working all day, he insisted on setting up the train set so my son could enjoy it right away.

This was a special moment and a special time in my life. I will never forget my friend's kindness and love and remember it when times get tough. He was such a lifesaver and relieved our stress and made life so much nicer that holiday season and he will never be forgotten. It wasn't the gifts but the fact that he thought enough of us to make us a part of his holiday and that made us feel important.

There are heroes out in the world that come into our lives just when we need them and we need to keep this in mind during times of stress.

Knowing you are loved gives you great strength and is like a life preserver keeping us afloat when we feel like giving up.

Next time you are feeling stressed out take a walk enjoying and savoring every moment. Take the time to notice the green trees, the wonderful woodsy smells, the mist and breeze on your face as you walk. Get totally lost in the moment. Enjoy nature at its best and just close your eyes and let it sweep you away from your daily stress, worries, and work and just relax into this wonderful and peaceful setting. Let go of the tension and take some time to just "be," and know that you are loved and that help will be there when you need it.

In our hurried world, we can never get enough of this time out. Because of this, we age faster, have serious health problems, overeat, smoke and drink too much. We try to get a fast fix from harmful substances instead of getting back to nature and let the natural environment sooth us.

Another good stress reliever that works for me is reliving the best days of my life. Reliving them over again brings me joy, raises my self-esteem and gives me a renewed sense of hope and fulfillment.

When I was about six years old, my father would take me on his bicycle for long, adventurous rides. He had an old, red bicycle and I would sometimes sit on the middle bar or on the handlebars and he would take me riding with him. This was such a special time for me.

My dad worked very hard in the retail grocery business. He was a store manager who put in long hours. He didn't have much time to spend with us because there were five of us children, my mom and the house to take care of, which took up most of any spare time he had. This is why these bike rides were extra special treats.

I would jump up on the middle bar and we would take off down the street. It seemed like we were going so fast like flying in the air but safer and I loved it! It was scary, exciting and so much fun feeling the wind in my face, blowing my hair and making me feel so very alive.

We would ride past farms, the woods and all of these fascinating houses. No two were alike and some were very old, made of brick and stone. A few were crudely put together and almost looked haunted to me and I imagined that ghosts inhabited them at night. I had a wild imagination as a child and these bike rides fed this immensely.

We would go through our neighborhoods and over a bridge where our local creek flowed. We would get off of the bike and walk along the creek, looking for fish in the water, frogs, turtles and other critters. This was one of my favorite things to do, walk along the water with my dad. When we would get to the bridge, I would peer underneath it where it was dark and ominous. I imagined trolls living there which frightened me but also added to the mystery and adventure of the trip.

At the far end of town, before we would turn back for home, we would approach the railroad tracks. The Soo Line Railroad went through our town bringing fruit, vegetables, manufactured items and other products for people to buy. There were always interesting characters that would hang out around the tracks and depot. Railway workers who were usually a tough looking bunch, dirty, unshaven, with deeply wrinkled skin. They were tan and weathered from being outdoors much of the time. I found them an interesting group to watch. I wondered about all of the adventures they must have had and the many places they had seen. I envied them for the freedom they possessed riding the railroad without ties or responsibilities, but I also thought of the loneliness that was part of their nomadic lifestyle. They had to give up a lot for this freedom and some not by choice.

There were also bums or hobos, as they called them at the time. Some were sleeping off last night's drinking binge and others were just waiting around for the next train to come by for their free ride. They were such a diverse group, so unlike the people I knew. Many seemed weary, depressed and had faces that would just stare blankly at me. Somehow I wanted to help them but didn't quite know how. I worried, even as a child, that someday that could be me.

I don't know how far we went on these bicycle rides, but I used to call them seven-milers. That is what it seemed like, but they really were much longer and farther than I thought at my young age. We would end our ride back home and did one big circle that was in our neighborhood called Indian Park Estates. It was called by this name because our homes were built over an old American Indian burial ground. I found this very fascinating as a child. I believed that the Indian's spirits still inhabited our area and felt their presence. I became interested in their culture and history because I lived in this area.

The bicycle rides were an important part of my childhood. I learned and experienced so much on them and got to spend this very precious and special time with my father that will stay with me forever. When I go back and relive this time of my life, it makes me smile, knowing that I was important enough for my dad to take this time out to be with me and getting to experience the wonders of our neighborhood and town.

Another moment I like to relive is the day I received my college degree. It was such an empowering day. It was a culmination of many hours of work during difficult and demanding times. Accomplishing this goal was an important event and holding that degree in my hands made me prouder than I ever had been in my life.

I completed two years of college in my twenties but was more interested in getting out into the working world and wanted to make money. School was boring and tedious to me and I felt it was time to get on with life as an adult instead of as a student.

After being out in the work world for a while, I realized how important the college degree was to career and personal success. I realized that I should have gotten it and finished when I had the chance early on. I somehow felt less fulfilled without it and kept it in mind as a goal.

I waited to go back to school when my son had reached thirteen years of age. I felt comfortable going to school at night when he was old enough to care for himself for a few hours.

When I went to register for school, I found out that many of the credits I had earned in my twenties would not transfer over, so it was almost like starting over. I was very discouraged at the time and almost gave up my goal. I am very thankful that I didn't and pursued it with a sense that failure was not acceptable.

I remember staying up until two o'clock in the morning working to finish papers that were due. I was working full-time, raising my son and taking two or three courses per semester pushing myself to accomplish this goal.

It was a very hot and humid day in May of 1987 when I actually went through the graduation ceremony. I bought myself a beautiful dress that cost over two hundred dollars. This was much more money than I usually paid for a dress, but this occasion was so special to me and I wanted to look my best. I felt I had earned it and deserved it for all the work I had put into getting my college degree.

The school I attended made us go to the ceremony even though I had one class left to complete. They only put on a graduation ceremony two times per year, in May and January and I did not want to wait until January to get my diploma. If I attended the ceremony in May, I could pick up my diploma in August after I successfully completed my final class.

I had to wait to get my actual diploma. At the ceremony in May, they only gave me a blank presentation folder. I had mixed feelings about attending but I am glad I did. It was exciting going up on the stage after hearing my name and I knew that nothing would stop me from finishing the final class so I enjoyed the moment and celebrated the fact that I had accomplished so much thus far.

That August day, when I actually picked up my college diploma, was such an important and life-changing event for me. I had achieved a goal and realized a dream and my heart and soul filled with a joy and a sense of pride. My self-esteem was at its highest and I return to this day whenever I am faced with a tough project or when my self-esteem is low. I relive those feelings I had that day and it renews my spirit and motivates me to carry on and accomplish more.

I relive other pleasures that were just special times in my life. When I was married, many years ago, my in-laws had a vacation home in Wisconsin on a canal. It was a wonderful A-frame structure with a large, white stone fireplace in the center that went all the way up from the floor to the ceiling. The second story was a loft and it was such a treat to get out of the city and visit this place on long weekends.

In the summer we would go out on a motorboat from the canals to the lake. It was very large, blue and filled with fish, mostly large mouth bass. Right around Mother's Day the large mouth bass run would come in and we would all pile in the boat to catch some fish. The fish came in to spawn and were so plentiful only at this time of the year.

When we would get out on the lake, there would be so many boats and fishermen. It was a sight to behold. All these people wanted to take advantage of this short window of fun and sport.

We would find a good spot and then cast out, hoping for a bite and then it would start. Every cast we made we would get a fish. We would end up with 30 or more fish in the boat and be exhausted but exhilarated by the fun we had that day.

Then we departed for the A-frame and put newspaper down on the kitchen floor and cleaned the fish. It was a messy job but we had lots of laughs and fun and we knew a delicious meal would follow. It was well worth it and thinking about this brings such warm memories.

My son was small at the time, maybe about three or four years old, but all of the fun, excitement and activity kept him occupied and even he enjoyed the experience immensely.

In the winter, at this vacation home, we would go snowmobiling. We had powerful Poloron snowmobiles and wore black padded jumpsuits to keep warm and protective helmets on our heads.

We rode the snowmobiles across the frozen lake through deep snow, with the engines loudly grinding and the rush of wind and snow in our faces. This was very exciting and what a great way to relieve stress and get out into the natural environment away from all the hustle and bustle of the work world.

Part of these trips would be a stop at a local restaurant where we would line up our helmets on a shelf with the rest of the snowmobilers' helmets and settle down to have some great food and a few beers.

It was fun watching people come in with their suits and helmets. You couldn't tell the men from the women until they took them off. It was unique to see all of the different ages of people who really enjoyed this sport. I was happy to see so many older, retired people there enjoying themselves.

These were wonderful breaks that we got during the winter when, in Chicago, it got cloudy, cold and dreary and you could really get down and depressed waiting for some sunshine to brighten your day. By getting away to the A-frame, we got a little break and some fun times that I recall from time to time when I need to escape.

These are just a few ideas on how you can relieve stress. Protect yourself from its negative effects by trying them. It is one of the best things you can do for yourself.

11

LIVE IN THE MOMENT

Too many of us dwell too much on the past or contemplate our future and we miss out on living in the moment.

It doesn't really serve a purpose to dwell on what happened or what we did in the past. We sometimes spend too much time beating ourselves up over mistakes we have made or jobs we should have taken, broken relationships and missed opportunities. It is much better to learn from these past experiences and take something constructive from them.

What can we learn from a mistake we made? Did we get ourselves trapped in a mountain of debt that may have taken years to get out from under? Maybe we learned to save before buying things instead of charging it. Maybe we learned to ask ourselves, "Do I really need this?" Think of all the junk you have lying around that you just had to have when the urge struck and later you ended up giving it away or throwing it in the garbage.

What can a relationship gone wrong teach us? Could we have selected the wrong partner? Perhaps we were just latching onto someone out of our fear of being alone. Did we transfer the responsibility of paying our bills or taking care of ourselves to someone else because we were not willing to do this ourselves? We could learn to be more loving and less demanding. We could learn to take on the responsibility for our own lives, expenses and well-being and not put this burden on anyone else. We could also learn to take the time to really get to know someone before leaping into life together on the whim that you are "madly in love." Love takes time and true love is more than hormones and chemistry. It is a respect that grows from working together to help one another. Bonds are formed and compatibility is tested and learned.

Learn to appreciate what you have right now in this moment. What can you enjoy with your family, friends or just by yourself? Forget about your worries and concentrate on just today. Close everything else out. This takes some practice because many of us are so used to planning and busying ourselves lest we might have to stop and face the present. That might be too painful, scary or maybe wonderful if you try. It is up to you to decide.

Watching movies forces me to live in the moment. I can get totally lost when I do this enjoyable pastime. I get transported away to the world in the story and leave everything else behind. I have strong powers of concentration and not much distracts me when I am watching a movie.

Find something that you can do to just keep you in the moment. When thoughts of the past or worries about the future come into your mind, banish them. With enough practice you can replace them with thoughts of enjoyment of just this point in time and nothing else.

12

HAVE AN ADVENTURE

As children we go out into the outside to play and can't wait to go on adventures. We create them in our minds and play them out like my brother Tom and I used to do when we were very young. We made believe that we were cowboys. I was Tex and he was Dave and we would ride our make-believe horses and save the West from the bad guys. We were also pirates and sailed out and captured treasure. We dressed up in mom and dad's clothing, me in high heels clopping down the sidewalk and he in suit coat, tie and Panama hat. What a sight to behold! We would visit our neighbor Lucille who would give us candy. This was like found treasure for us!

When we grow up we get so busy with life, just working and raising our families that we lose our sense of adventure and need to rekindle it.

Adventures can be found all around us. Creating it doesn't have to cost a lot of money or take up all of your time, but you must be sure to set aside some time in your busy life for adventure.

Take a moment to think back to what excited you as a child. You can use this to decide on what kind of adventure you want to embark on today.

I loved to explore the outdoors as a child and love to create adventure by going to new places where I have never been before. Nature had played a large role in the adventures I had as a child and also still does with my adult adventures.

Even the neighborhood I live in is adventurous. It's like a biology lesson each time I go outdoors. I was riding my bicycle just the other day and saw a six-foot long alligator up on all four legs, completely out of the water, on the grassy shoreline of one of the lakes on the golf course in my neighborhood. He looked like he was ready to go chase after something and I was looking right at him from about twenty feet away!

I was afraid and excited at the same time. It is rare to see an alligator up and out of the water like this one. Usually they hide in the water or are lazing on the shore warming themselves in the sun and are not very active. This one must have been really hungry and spotted some food. I was hoping it wasn't me!

I marveled at how nice and clean he was and how beautiful his belly was radiant with shiny white ridges. I didn't hang around too long though but tried to pedal away in a hurry. My legs felt like lead weights from the fear it may come after and attack me. For the most part, alligators are not aggressive but this one was ready for action!

Another time, while rounding the corner on the street where I live, I spotted a large soft-shelled turtle with his pointy nose crossing the street. I stopped to watch him and enjoy how wondrous a creature he was. I used to only see pictures of these animals in my Reptiles & Amphibians books in Chicago as a child. How wonderful to see them now in person.

How do you find adventure? It's around every corner or you can seek it out. Think back on what you did as a child to create adventure and do it again as an adult.

I had a fantastic little adventure recently right in my own city. We have a very large flea market in town and I hadn't been there in years. I woke up early on a Sunday morning and decided to go there.

It is such a great place to have an adventure because there is so much to see and sample. Even before you go inside there are produce stands outside selling the most beautiful fruits and vegetables you've ever seen. All the sweet odors and bright colors are so attractive and make you salivate just being around such abundance.

I have my favorite vendors at the flea market. One is a t-shirt vendor that sells shirts five (5) for ten dollars ($10.00). I love a bargain and this is the best one ever! I rummage through the racks and always find some great shirts with silk-screened animals, seashells, fish, sports teams and other designs. I buy smaller sizes to wear with jeans or shorts and larger sizes to wear to bed and for just relaxing around the house.

Then I hit the makeup and perfume vendors. I love makeup and like to try new eye shadows and lipsticks and always find items for fifty cents (.50) and one dollar ($1.00) that may have originally sold for thirty to one hundred dollars. Some are discontinued items or last season's colors, but who cares or even knows that you are wearing last year's colors. I love them anyway!

Next are the jewelry vendors. I love the ones that sell the quality copies and "fakes" of jewelry popular on the home shopping network television shows. The vendors at the flea market sell for one half or less than the prices on television. I've scored beautiful bracelets and rings at these tables and get many compliments from my friends and co-workers on my selections.

Another great attraction at the flea market are all of the animals. There are vendors with the most beautiful exotic birds, puppies, cats, reptiles and even some livestock such as goats and sheep. I have so much fun petting them and talking to the animals and the vendors asking all sorts of questions and learning about feeding them, their personalities and different traits and getting to know the vendors too. Most of them started out owning the animals as a hobby and turned it into a business and had fun doing it too.

Do you know that giant iguanas love to have their back pointy spikes petted lightly? One of the vendors had me try this when he saw me admiring his large pet iguana. It was about three feet long and a foot high and I never saw one so large. He told me to run my fingers on the tips of the soft spikes on the iguana's back and the iguana just went all silly and mushy with delight. He closed his eyes and put his head down and proceeded to be lulled to sleep by my touch. I would have never guessed this behavior from the iguana and decided that despite their formidable appearance, they were quite lovely creatures after all.

Let's not forget to mention all of the tasty food this flea market had to offer. From home made Mexican delights such as enchiladas and menudo to burgers and freshly made potato chips the wonderful smells and sights are worth the trip just to get the chance to savor and taste these sensations.

Fresh lemonade, orange juice smoothies, root beer floats and funnel cakes are just some of the other delights to be found on this adventure.

At the end of my day at the "flea" I always stop at the flower vendor to get a bouquet for home. This time it was bright yellow spider mums from Colombia for two dollars a dozen. What a great bargain and you can't get a deal like that anywhere else. I brought them home and they brightened my surroundings for a week.

This was such a great little adventure, close to home, very inexpensive and a day I will cherish and remember for a long time.

13

NEVER TAKE ANYTHING FOR GRANTED

My father's passing a few years ago taught me a very valuable lesson. He woke up the morning of his last day and didn't know that this was his final time in this life.

How would he have lived differently had he known this ahead of time? What would he have done differently, who would he have made a point of seeing and what would he have said to them?

I thought about this often after he died and I felt like he was sending me a powerful message. Get out there and really live your life to the fullest and never waste a moment or take anything for granted. You never know when your last day will come. Quit whining about what you don't have and concentrate on what you do have and give something back to society. Leave a legacy and make a difference, no matter how small, before you leave this place.

Cherish the people you have in your life that are good to you and don't be afraid to let them know how you feel about them. Tell them what wonderful people they are and how you feel treasured to have them in your life. Give them hugs and if you can't be with them, tell them you are sending them one through the telephone or in a letter.

My dad's hugs, the last year of his life, were different. It was as if he knew his time was limited and they were longer, warmer and more heartfelt than ever before. I noticed this but just figured he somehow cherished me more now that he was older, but later I found out that his doctor had told him something during one of his checkups that made him cry. This may have been that his health was failing and he knew that he had to make every hug and every minute count.

Don't let picky, petty arguments or disagreements keep you separated from others. Get over them, forgive and move on. Life is too short and too precious to waste holding grudges and dwelling on hurtful, negative behaviors.

Remove the toxic or abusive people from your life by not associating with them or by lessening their impact on your life. Don't internalize their attacks, but hear what they are saying, see if there is any truth to it and change what you can to improve your relationships by listening carefully to what they are telling you.

Let's face it, there are those people out there that you will never be friends with and maybe you have to deal with them from time to time. Use some understanding and try to find a common ground and put some effort into it. You may see them come around before long. If not, at least you will know that you did your best and tried to make it work out.

Let those people you love know it every day. Communicate this through words, actions and do it often. Don't be afraid of doing this. People need to know and be reassured. We all have times when we need a boost and a compliment, an I love you or just an affirming statement like *you're the greatest* can really make someone's day and make them feel better just knowing someone cares about them and appreciates them. This is such a powerful tool that you can use to really make a difference in other's lives.

Don't take the things you have for granted or try to compare what you have to others. We spend much of our time lamenting the fact that we may not have as much money as we would like or the greatest career, largest most expensive house or car, wear designer clothes and frequent fancy country clubs and restaurants.

These things are fine but they don't really make a huge difference in how you feel about yourself. Only you can do that. Obviously, having enough money to live is important, but needing millions of dollars is not necessary for happiness.

It is all right to strive to do your best but this does not always result in success and money. When this happens, many people become disappointed, give up or become depressed. This is very understandable and I have been through this myself. Instead you should appreciate the fact that you are doing your best and take a look at what you do have. Give yourself a pat on the back each day for just hanging in there and making it this far no matter what situation you are in at the moment. Don't take what you have for granted. You could be in worse shape financially, physically, emotionally and spiritually. Focus on the positive aspects of your life and try to take a proactive approach to those negative aspects.

Let's say you have a wonderful family life but maybe your job isn't the greatest. Focus on your family and realize that sometimes a job is just a way to earn money until you can find that dream career. Go to work each day with a smile on your face and a positive attitude knowing that this job is giving you the money you need to take care of and enjoy your family.

Remember that you are the one that controls your attitude and going in to work with a bad one does not make you an effective worker. It also will eventually affect your health in a negative way. This negativity will cause you to have conflicts with others in the workplace too. You will have a tendency to overeat, eat the wrong kinds of foods, suffer indigestion, heartburn, high blood pressure and headaches due to the stress the negativity causes. Over time it takes a heavy toll on your body and you may ruin your health.

Conflict with others at work makes it difficult for everyone and can even get you fired. When you come in with a negative attitude you are difficult to deal with and the lines of communication break down. You cannot effectively get the job done if there is poor communication. When no one wants to deal with you because you might bite their head off, you won't know what needs to be done, when, how and where the projects are heading.

Learn to work together to get the work completed and focus on the task and not on the fact that this may not be the greatest job in the world or the best place to work. Realize that you are a vital part of this process and you have a responsibility to your boss and co-workers to do your best to keep the flow of work going. By being cooperative and supportive of your co-workers, assisting them also to do their best just makes it such a better and more successful operation. Seeing your impact on how this affects everything can give you that positive feeling you need to be satisfied even in a job that may not be your dream job.

Don't take your job for granted. It could be gone tomorrow and you could be facing debt, uncertainty, depression, loss of self-esteem and the loss of your family. Keep in mind that a job isn't your life. You should be defined by the person you are and your contributions to your family and society and not just by the work you do.

Speaking of contributions, what have you done to give back to society? Do you know that giving back can give you the greatest satisfaction of all?

Volunteering to help others can give you the greatest joy and sense of satisfaction. I learned this when I got actively involved when I became a member of a county steering committee for a charitable organization here in Florida.

The first rally I attended really opened my eyes to the support that is needed in our area for charitable work. I met a small boy, two-years old who was severely handicapped and challenged. He had braces on his legs and yet he couldn't wait to run up to the people in the audience and give them hugs. He had this big smile on his face and was such a joy to behold. He didn't know he was any different from anyone else.

His parents spoke of the challenges they had with finding a school for him because he could be out of control at times. They felt lucky to have found one right in the city where they lived. This school was partially funded by the State and partially through donations received from the community. The school had one-on-one contact with the students that provided the necessary education and skills that this little boy needed in order to thrive and develop.

It also provided a support system for his parents, giving them a break from all of their responsibilities taking care of him on a daily basis.

These schools and other organizations need volunteers to get involved in keeping them running and finding donors to provide the income necessary for their continuance.

From my involvement with this charitable group, I got to see, hear stories from and visit the people who actually were assisted through our efforts. This was so rewarding to me to know that little old me could make a difference in the world. I could contribute not only in monetary terms, but give myself and my time to make things better for someone.

Why not try to find an organization in your area and give something back to society in appreciation for all you have received. It will help others and give you one of the greatest rewards you can ever imagine.

CONCLUSION

This book offers my insight on aging and living at fifty years and beyond. We baby boomers have always had the advantage of being a very large and influential group. Together we can change the negative stereotypes of being an older person in today's society.

By taking care of our health, keeping a sensible diet, exercising, taking care of our finances and lessening our stress while having adventures, we can live active and very positive lives well beyond our middle years.

Never have another negative thought about aging. There are so many benefits to it and you are only limited by thoughts that others have thrust upon us. Don't buy into it or take any disrespect because you are older. Keep in mind that those who look down on us now will travel this road themselves someday.

Life is such a gift and is very fragile. Protect yours and live it with all of your being. You only get one chance to be in this adventure. Remember not to waste it or take it for granted.

A FINAL THOUGHT

As baby boomers we have lived through amazing times, seen wondrous events and experienced both joy and hardships. We look upon ourselves as survivors, innovators, lovers of beauty, culture with hopes and dreams for grand futures. Our spirit and numbers are so strong that we have influenced everything we touch and our influence will live on in our families and what we leave behind. There will never be another baby boomer generation and we can savor this uniqueness knowing that we will always be remembered as the generation that followed the great war and built this nation.

BIBLIOGRAPHY

1. Ray, Mitra. <u>From Here to Longevity</u>. Seattle: Shining Star Publishing, 2002.

2. Null, Gary. <u>Gary Null's Ultimate Anti-Aging Pro</u>gram. New York: Kensington Books, 1999.

3. Chopra, Deepak, M.D. <u>Grow Younger, Live Long</u>er. New York: Harmony Books, 2001.

4. Trudeau, Kevin. <u>Natural Cures They Don't Want You to Know About</u>. Hinsdale: Alliance Publishing Group, Inc., 2004.

5. Agatston, Arthur, M.D. <u>The South Beach Diet</u>. New York: Random House, 2003.

6. Orman, Suze. <u>The 9 Steps to Financial Freedom</u>. New York: Three Rivers Press, 1997.

7. Weil, Andrew, M.D. <u>Eating Well For Optimum Health</u>. New York: Alfred A. Knopf, 2000.

8. Covey, Stephen R. <u>The 7 Habits of Highly Effective People</u>. New York: Simon & Schuster, Inc., 1990.

9. Dyer, Wayne, <u>Dr. How To Be A No-Limit Person</u>. Niles: Nightingale-Conant Corporation, cassette tapes, 1987.

10. Downes, John and Goodman, Elliot. <u>Barron's Finance and Investment Handbook</u>. New York: Barron's Educational Series, Inc., 1987.

11. Robbins, Anthony. <u>Unlimited Power</u>. New York: Robbins Research Institute, Fireside, 1986, 1997.

RESOURCES

1. **Elizabeth Arden Visible Difference Face Cream**—purchase at major department store such as Macys, Dillards, Nordstroms or see their website at: **http://www.elizabetharden.com**

2. **Key West Aloe Night Moist Cream**—find locations or purchase on their website at: **http://www.keywestaloe.com/**

3. **Aloe Moisturizing Crème with Vitamins E, A & D**—find this product at many health food stores or contact the manufacturer, Prime Natural Health Labs, Carson, CA 90749-5308

4. **Estee Lauder Face Creams and Equalizer Makeup**—Purchase at major department stores such as Macys, Dillards, Nordstroms, or see their website at: **http://www.esteelauder.com**

5. **Revlon Age Defying Makeup**—purchase this line of makeup at Walgreens Drug Stores, Wal-Mart, K-Mart, Target, CVS and other fine drug stores.

6. **Signature Club A**—purchase this line of makeup by Adrien Arpel at the Home Shopping Network website: **http://www.hsn.com**

7. **Aziza Eyeshadows**—purchase this product at Walgreens Drug Stores, Wal-Mart, K-Mart, Target, CVS and other fine drug stores.

8. **Smashbox Brow Tech**—purchase this product at: **http://www.qvc.com**

9. **Fleamasters Flea Market, 4135 Dr. M.L. King, Jr. Blvd., Fort Myers, FL 33916. Telephone 239-334-7001**

10. **Naples, Florida**—for information on beaches and places to stay visit the following website: **http://www.napleschamber.org/index.asp**

11. **Sanibel, Florida**—visit the city's official website at: **http://www.mysanibel.com/**

12. **Captiva, Florida**—for information on beaches and places to stay: **http://www.sanibel-captiva.org/index.asp**

You may contact the author, Mary Christofano at: **mchristofano@comcast.net**

She is available to call in to Book Clubs and is available for presentations, book signings and seminars upon request.

978-0-595-41703-2
0-595-41703-5

www.ingramcontent.com/pod-product-compliance
Lightning Source LLC
Chambersburg PA
CBHW051432280526
45785CB00003B/1252